DUKAN
EVERYDAY
EASY
COOKBOOK

Dr Pierre Dukan & Joy Skipper

First published in Great Britain in 2013 by Hodder & Stoughton
An Hachette UK company

1

Copyright © Joy Skipper and Dr Pierre Dukan 2013

Photography Copyright © Lis Parsons 2013

A CIP catalogue record for this title is available from the British Library

Hardback ISBN 978 1 444 77682 9
Ebook ISBN 978 1 444 77683 6

Typeset in Miller

Printed and bound in Germany by Mohn media

Hodder & Stoughton policy is to use papers that are natural, renewable and recyclable
products and made from wood grown in sustainable forests. The logging and
manufacturing processes are expected to conform to the environmental regulations
of the country of origin.

Hodder & Stoughton Ltd
338 Euston Road
London NW1 3BH
www.hodder.co.uk

Designer & Art Director: **Kate Barr**
Photographer: **Lis Parsons**
Food Stylist: **Joy Skipper**
Props Stylist: **Liz Hippisley**
Copyeditor: **Kay Halsey**
Project Editor: **Sarah Hammond**
Editorial Director: **Nicky Ross**

CONTENTS

FOREWORD 4

INTRODUCTION 6

TOP 10 ATTACK 18

LUNCH BOX 38

SOUPS, SNACKS & STARTERS 62

CHICKEN (& OTHER BIRDS) TONIGHT 86

MEATY MEALS 104

FISH FAVOURITES 126

MEAT-FREE FEASTS 156

FRIENDS FOR DINNER 186

DESSERTS 208

BAKING 242

INDEX 253

FOREWORD

My career as a doctor and nutritionist has mostly been spent helping people tackle weight problems. Seeking pleasure from food as a way of neutralizing the difficulty of getting pleasure from other areas in our lives is an effective survival strategy, but one that makes us put on weight, so aiding men and women who eat to find comfort from their food is never straightforward.

It's simply a law of life that whenever we experience something negative, difficult and annoying or something that makes us suffer, our whole being tries to soften the shock by seeking out its exact opposite, by recreating something positive and easy that will give us pleasure and satisfaction. The medical term for this is homeostasis. Without being aware of it, there is an automatic control inside us compelling us to correct whatever it is, disguised as suffering or lack of pleasure, which is telling us we are straying away from the norms we are biologically adapted to.

Seen this way, seeking out pleasure is no longer mere hedonistic luxury but simply a way of regaining our lost equilibrium. And as we try and tackle weight problems, which have become a public health issue in the UK and around the world, being able to cook attractive, mouth-watering dishes can be a great support to anyone who wants to watch their weight without sacrificing quality of life.

Before we get to these recipes, which you will find surprisingly easy and totally delicious, I would like to draw your attention to something about which the general public and many doctors seem quite unaware. The current crisis, epidemic even, of so many people becoming overweight that we see as inevitable and existing since time immemorial is in fact a recent occurrence. It even has a date of birth: 1944. People were indeed overweight or obese before the war, but they did not form a particular group within the population. Just sixteen years later, in 1960, the figures showed that there were one million overweight people in France. Nowadays that number has risen to 27 million and this mirrors the growth in other countries around the world. There has to be an end to this unstoppable upsurge in weight problems and this book is one of the tools we need to block its advance.

My method has travelled far and wide. Starting off in France, it has now permeated many different cultures with their own foods and cuisine. It comes with its four phases and its 100 Eat As Much As You Want Foods. Twenty of them may vary depending on the culture and climate but eighty are always available, they are universal. Tomatoes, salmon, chicken, eggs, yoghurt, carrots – mankind's food heritage is made up of these foodstuffs. And an infinite variety and great array of dishes can be created from these fundamental foods.

So today let me introduce you to Joy Skipper's cuisine. She has filled me with enthusiasm. Her cuisine is British cuisine, but just like foods, artists can be universal too. And when it's good, the colours of the different flags merge together.

My thanks go to Joy for having so cleverly managed to get across in this velvet glove the iron hand of my message.

Dr Pierre Dukan

INTRODUCTION

The Dukan Diet was first published in France in 2001, after a number of years of improving and adjusting the comprehensive programme that was originally devised by Dr Pierre Dukan for his general-practice patients. The diet is now used by an ever-growing number of people aiming to control their weight.

For those people trying to lose weight, there is a huge number of diets to choose from, and I know it can be overwhelming deciding which one to choose. The Dukan Diet is not a short-term plan. The intention is that, once the weight is lost and you have reached your True Weight (discover your True Weight at www.dukandiet.com), there is a healthy eating plan that enables you to consolidate the loss and never put the pounds back on.

There are four phases of the Dukan Diet and each is well planned and simple to follow. Once you know the rules and the foods you are allowed, you can eat as much of them as you like! There is so much pleasure in watching the weight disappear, whilst having the joy of eating great food each day.

The diet is based around two main food groups — foods rich in animal proteins and vegetables. When our species came into being, man was designed to hunt, to pursue game and catch fish, whilst women concentrated on gathering whatever foods they could find, especially plants. These became the foundation foods of the human diet. But since that time, our lifestyles have changed, as have the foods we eat. We now eat more for pleasure than as a way of getting nutrition. Sugar was once thought to be a luxury, but now sugar and fat are in our foods in abundance — with the resulting increase in obesity worldwide.

The four phases of the Dukan Diet are designed to guide the dieter to their desired weight and then keep them there. The four successive diets, which gradually include more foods, have been specifically devised to bring about the following results in the following order: The first (**Attack**) phase gives a lightning start and an intense and stimulating weight loss. The second (**Cruise**) phase provides a steady, regular weight loss that takes you straight to your desired weight. Phase three (**Consolidation**) consolidates your weight loss and lasts for a period of five days for every pound lost. The final phase (**Stabilization**) is a permanent lifetime eating plan that includes three simple rules to ensure the weight remains lost.

As with all eating plans, it is necessary to be organized and to think ahead about what you are going to eat, thereby preventing any lapses that would mean going back to the beginning again. I find the great thing with this diet is that there is no counting of calories (or any other units) to worry about, but making sure you know which foods you are allowed for each phase is important. Once you have mastered this, you will find your meal planning and preparation become second nature.

The first step to being organized is to ensure that your store cupboard, fridge and freezer are stocked with the foods you are allowed from the start of the diet (see the Attack list on page 11):

PROTEINS

You can choose from:

- lean meats
- poultry
- fish and seafood
- eggs
- tofu
- fat-free or low-fat dairy products

Filling your fridge with good lean meats, fresh fish and seafood will ensure you always have good protein to hand. Eggs and fat-free dairy products can also be used, and are perfect for making sweet dishes if you have a sweet tooth.

FLAVOURINGS

From the very beginning of the diet you can choose from flavourings such as:

- herbs
- spices
- chillies
- onions
- spring onions
- chives
- shallots
- garlic
- ginger
- lemon grass
- vinegar
- capers
- tomato purée
- mustard
- horseradish
- soy sauce
- Worcestershire sauce
- sweetener
- lemon zest & juice
- lime zest & juice
- orange zest
- orange flower water
- vanilla

These flavourings are highly recommended. Using them brings out the flavour of foods and heightens their sensory value, thereby encouraging you to eat a wide variety of foods regularly. Baking powder, low-salt stock cubes, gelatine and agar-agar can also be used to give your dishes more variety and texture. And at www.mydukandietshop.co.uk you will find the full range of Dukan flavourings to help you make the most of your food.

OAT BRAN

Oat bran is the fibrous husk that surrounds and protects the oat grain. The grain, used to make rolled oats, is rich in simple sugars, whilst oat bran has few simple sugars, but is very rich in proteins and particularly soluble fibres. Oat bran also has the ability to absorb 25 times its volume of water, which means that as it reaches the stomach, it swells and give a feeling of fullness. Many recipes in this book include oat bran to help you achieve your daily intake (see page 9) but it is just as simple to whisk it into a drink or soup or sprinkle it over your scrambled egg or salad.

WATER

The other important part of this diet is water. The more water you drink, the more you urinate, and the greater the opportunity for the kidneys to flush out toxins from the breakdown of unwanted fats and hormones. Mineral water is recommended, but if you prefer tap water, that is fine too.

COOKING AT HOME

I have been writing about food for over twenty years and cooking has always been a passion of mine. To me, the best meal is a home-cooked one, where you know exactly what has gone into the food on your plate. This is why the Dukan recipes are so important. I thought writing recipes for the diet would be a real challenge, but once I understood the concept and realized what a great range of wonderful fish and vegetables could be included, it became easy, and exciting! And, as with most recipes, the simplest ones are usually the best, as long as you start with good-quality ingredients.

The recipes in this book have a particularly vital role to play during the first two phases (**Attack** and **Cruise**), which is to offer pleasure, flavour and variety, and to satisfy hunger, thus giving you a boost to get to your goal weight. And remember, there is no limit to the amount of these foods you can eat, so there is no reason ever to feel hungry.

If you have a look through the book, you will get an idea of how you can use the many foods allowed to make great meals, not only for you, but for the whole family. If you are on the diet, but the rest of the family is not, you can adjust the recipes to suit all of you, so you don't have to cook separate meals every night! Lots of the recipes in this book will work for everyone.

Some recipes can also be used in more than one phase and some can be tweaked to be enjoyed by those on the diet, or not. Use the recipes to have as varied a diet as possible, with as many flavours as possible, to enable you to stave off the boredom normally experienced on other diets. Enjoying your food with family and friends is one of life's great pleasures and, even if you are following the Dukan principles, the recipes in this book should help you to do just that.

THE DUKAN METHOD
THE MAIN PRINCIPLES
This tried-and-tested method is based on a certain number of key principles.

4 PHASES TO ACHIEVE RAPID AND LASTING WEIGHT LOSS

Phase 1: Attack (pure proteins, PP)
Only natural, pure proteins are eaten in this phase of your diet. Attack gets going with lightning speed and your weight loss will be very quick.

Phase 2: Cruise (alternating between pure proteins, PP, and proteins + vegetables, PV)
After the Attack period, when you waged war on your surplus pounds, comes a Cruise period, during which you follow a diet of alternating proteins. Your meals will consist of proteins one day, then vegetables and proteins the next. This way you will reach your target weight.

Phase 3: Consolidation

Consolidation is when you gradually reintroduce foods that have so far been banned. Once you have got down to the weight you want, it is important to avoid the rebound phenomenon; after any rapid weight loss the body tends to pile back on the lost pounds extremely quickly. So this is an especially tricky period and your diet is by no means at an end. For every pound you lose, you will need to remain five days in the Consolidation phase.

Phase 4: Stabilization

The permanent Stabilization period is just as crucial since it is decisive in determining the success of your diet. So that you do not regain any of the weight you have lost, you will need to apply three simple measures throughout your life. In particular, one day a week you will have to follow a pure protein diet, preferably every Thursday. These protein Thursdays will protect you from regaining weight.

FOR ZERO FRUSTRATION, 100 'AS MUCH AS YOU WANT' FOODS

There is absolutely no need to weigh any food with this method. You can eat as much as you want of all the foods that are allowed. The Attack phase, when you are allowed 72 proteins only, does not last very long. You will very quickly move into the Cruise phase with its 28 vegetables, when you are allowed 100 foods.

OAT BRAN

This is the method's star food and one of the healthiest foodstuffs there is. Oat bran aids digestion; it makes you feel full and satisfied; it reduces your cholesterol level and helps to protect you from diabetes and cancer of the colon. You will eat oat bran throughout the diet in varying quantities:

Phase 1: Attack – 1½ tablespoons per day
Phase 2: Cruise – 2 tablespoons per day
Phase 3: Consolidation – 2½ tablespoons per day
Phase 4: Stabilization – 3 tablespoons per day

REGULAR EXERCISE

You don't have to join a gym to follow this diet. All you need to do is include a minimum amount of exercise in your daily routine — a 20–30-minute walk every day and walking up the stairs instead of taking the lift or escalator.

KEEP TO A MEALTIME PATTERN: With your meals, it is important that you stick to a routine otherwise you will end up feeling frustrated after a few days. Sitting down to eat and sharing a nice hot dish is always comforting and convivial. Of course, for the time being, your meal will consist of protein foods only. However, with the recipes that follow, you will discover how it is possible to come up with really tasty menus using just proteins. As you put your menus together according to what you enjoy eating, do try always to include a starter, a main dish and a pudding.

PHASE 1: ATTACK
(PURE PROTEINS, PP)

The pure proteins phase is lightning quick. By following it you will be in control of a mighty bulldozer that crushes all resistance in its path. So get on board!

AS MUCH PP AS YOU WANT

Of all the foodstuffs we eat, only egg white is made up of virtually pure proteins. However, there is a certain number of foods that come close to the perfection we are seeking. The following list includes foods that are extremely high in pure proteins, which are allowed during this first phase:

- beef (but not rib steak, rib or any cuts for stewing)
- veal
- poultry (except duck and goose)
- cooked ham slices (no fat or rind)
- fish
- crustaceans and shellfish
- eggs
- vegetable proteins
- fat-free dairy products

You can eat as much as you want of all these foods.

A SHORT PHASE TO ACHIEVE SPECTACULAR WEIGHT LOSS

This Attack phase is a real psychological turning point and surprise for your metabolism. It should enable you to shed quickly and effectively the maximum amount of weight your body is capable of losing during this brief time span. You will be surprised yourself by it.

How long it lasts will depend on how much weight you have to lose and how many diets you have previously tried. Here are a few pointers to help you set yourself a clear goal and stick to it:

Target weight loss	Phase 1 lasts
≤ 5kg (11lb)	1 day
≤ 10kg (22lb)	5 days
10–20kg (22–44lb)	5 days
≥ 20kg (44lb)	7 days (after seeking medical advice)

WALK

Go walking for at least 20 minutes every day.

WHAT CAN I EAT DURING ATTACK?

COOKED/CURED MEATS

Bresaola (air-dried beef
/wind-dried beef)
Cooked chicken/turkey
slices (without any fat
or rind)
Cooked ham slices
(without any fat or rind)

MEAT

Beef steak
Calf's liver
Chicken liver
Fillet of beef
Light bacon, max. 5% fat
Minced steak, max. 5% fat
Rabbit
Roast beef
Roast veal
Rump steak
Sirloin steak
Tongue (calf's and lamb's)
Veal chop
   (trimmed of any fat)
Veal escalope
Veal kidney
Venison

POULTRY

Chicken (without the skin)
Guinea fowl
Ostrich steak
Partridge
Pheasant
Pigeon
Poussin
Quail
Turkey

FISH

Cod (fresh)/Ling
Dab/Lemon sole
Dover sole
Fish roe (cod, salmon,
   herring, mullet)
Grey mullet
Haddock
Hake
Halibut
Herring
Mackerel
Monkfish
Plaice
Pollock/Coley
Rainbow/Salmon trout
Red mullet
Salmon/Smoked salmon
   (and smoked trout,
   haddock and eel)
Sardines
Sea bass
Sea bream
Seafood sticks (surimi)
Skate
Swordfish
Tuna (and tinned tuna
   in water or brine)
Turbot
Whiting

SEAFOOD

Calamari/Squid
Clams
Cockles
Crab
Crayfish
Dublin Bay prawns
Lobster
Mussels
Oysters

SEAFOOD CONT.

Prawns/Shrimps
Scallops
Whelks

EGGS

Hen's eggs
Quail's eggs

DAIRY PRODUCTS

Fat-free fromage frais
Fat-free Greek yoghurt
Fat-free natural yoghurt
   (plain or flavoured
   with sweetener)
Skimmed milk
   (fresh or powdered)
Virtually fat-free
   cottage cheese
Virtually fat-free quark

VEGETABLE PROTEINS

Konjac
Oat bran
Seitan
Tofu

PHASE 2: CRUISE
(ALTERNATING BETWEEN PP AND PV)

Those eagerly awaited vegetables are back on the menu again; you eat them on alternate days along with the pure proteins until you get down to your True Weight.

WEIGHT LOSS OVER THE LONG TERM

When you are in the alternating phase you will no doubt notice your weight loss slow down. This is quite normal as your body has to adjust to this new phase in order to take the diet in its stride over the long term.

Whereas your weight loss has so far been spectacular, all of a sudden your scales seem to be stuck. As soon as vegetables are reintroduced, so too is the water that a protein-only diet has artificially flushed out. The alternating phases are by definition less water-repellent than the pure protein phases. However, take heart. As your fat disappears, the weight you are losing is real enough; and, although it may be somewhat camouflaged by fluid gain, it is still going on without any problem.

Of course, on pure protein days you'll be delighted to see your scales point in the right direction again. As you get into your diet, you'll find it's like going down a flight of stairs — stagnation as you pause on a step, then suddenly you drop down to the next step, and so on.

How long should this phase last? That all depends on how many pounds you want to lose. It will last until you reach your target weight.

ALTERNATING PURE PROTEINS (PP) AND PROTEINS AND VEGETABLES (PV)

There are different ways of alternating, but the one that works best and with least frustration is the 1 PP day/1 PV day rhythm.

100 'AS MUCH AS YOU WANT' FOODS

You can continue eating as much as you want of the proteins you are allowed.

Now you will add certain vegetables to your menu: tomatoes, cucumber, radish, spinach, asparagus, leeks, French beans, cabbage, mushrooms, celery, fennel, all sorts of salad leaves, chicory, chard, aubergines, courgettes, peppers and even carrots and beetroot as long as you don't eat them at every meal.

You can eat as much as you want of these vegetables with no restriction on quantity but without overdoing it.

WALK

Your 'prescription' walk should now be extended to 30 minutes per day.

WHAT CAN I EAT DURING CRUISE?

You can eat all the proteins from the Attack phase on page 11, and you are also now allowed foods from the tolerated list below.

VEGETABLES

Artichoke (globe)
Asparagus
Aubergine
Beetroot
Broccoli/Purple sprouting broccoli
Brussels sprouts
Cabbage (red, white and green)
Carrot
Cauliflower
Celery/Celeriac
Chicory
Courgette
Cucumber
Fennel
French beans/String beans/Mangetout
Kohlrabi
Leek
Mushrooms
Onion
Palm hearts
Peppers
Pumpkin/Marrow/Squash
Radish
Rhubarb
Salad leaves
    (curly endive, lamb's lettuce etc.)
Soya beans
Spinach/Swiss chard
Tomato

TOLERATED FOODS

From Phase 2: Cruise, there is a certain number of basic foodstuffs and cooking aids that are deemed 'tolerated'.

• Do not exceed 2 portions per day.
• In Stabilization and Consolidation they are not allowed on your protein days.

Chicken sausages max, 10% fat (100g)
Cooking wine, for cooking without
    a lid (3 tablespoons or 30g)
Cornflour (1 tablespoon or 20g)
Crème fraîche, 3% fat
    (1 tablespoon or 30g)
Fat-free cordials (20ml)
Extra-light cream cheese, 7% fat (40g)
Fat-free fruit yoghurt (1 x 125g)
Fat-reduced, sugar-free cocoa powder
    11% fat (1 teaspoon or 7g)
Goji berries (1–3 tablespoons,
    depending on the phase)
Low-fat grated cheese, 7% fat (30g)
Merguez sausages,
    well pricked and well cooked (50g)
Oil (3 drops or 3ml)
Original fat-free Actimel (1 x 100g)
Plain soya yoghurt (1 x 125g)
Ready-to-use gazpacho soup
    (1 glass or 150ml)
Ricore chicory coffee (1 teaspoon or 7g)
Sesame seeds (1 teaspoon)
Soya flour (1 tablespoon or 20g)
Soya milk (1 glass or 150ml)
Sweetened soy sauce
    (1 teaspoon or 5ml)
Tempeh (50g)

PHASE 3: CONSOLIDATION

Once you have reached your True Weight, you must go through the Consolidation phase so that you don't put any weight back on.

FOR EVERY POUND LOST, YOU SPEND 5 DAYS IN CONSOLIDATION

The Consolidation phase is divided into two periods of equal length. If you have lost 10lb (4kg) you will have to stay in Consolidation 1 for 25 days, then 25 days in Consolidation 2. If you have lost 60lb (27kg), you will have to stick with Consolidation 1 for 150 days and then the same again in Consolidation 2. But don't worry: even if Consolidation is a tricky period, you can eat foods again that up until now were not allowed. So your menus will be more varied and there will plenty for you to enjoy.

REINTRODUCING FOODS THAT WERE NOT ALLOWED, BUT IN LIMITED QUANTITIES

As well as the protein foods and vegetables from the Cruise phase, certain foods are at last permitted again. However, you will have to follow a set of instructions that are specific enough to prevent you from losing control in any way.

- **1 portion of fruit per day (except grapes, bananas, cherries and dried fruit) in Consolidation 1, and 2 portions in Consolidation 2**
  = 1 apple, pear, orange, grapefruit, peach, nectarine, etc.
  = 1 dish of small fruit (e.g. strawberries, raspberries)
  = ½ much larger fruit (e.g. melon)
  = 2 medium-sized fruit (e.g. apricots, plums)

- **2 slices of wholemeal bread per day (50g)**
  You can eat them at any time of the day — for breakfast, as a lunchtime sandwich with cold meat or ham, or even in the evening with your portion of cheese.

- **40g mature cheese per day**
  You are allowed to eat all hard-rind cheeses such as Cheddar, Gouda, Comté, etc. For now, avoid fermented cheeses such as blue cheese, Camembert and goat's cheese. Take care to eat this portion in a single go, so that you avoid making mistakes with quantities and nibbling at extra cheese.

- **1 x 220g serving of starchy foods per week in Consolidation 1, and 2 servings in Consolidation 2**
  = Pasta (preferably wholemeal)
  = Couscous, polenta, bulgur wheat
  = Brown or wild rice
  = Lentils
  Avoid white rice and potatoes

- **1 portion of leg of lamb or roast pork fillet per week**

ONE OR TWO CELEBRATION MEALS PER WEEK

Once a week in Consolidation 1, and twice a week in Consolidation 2, you will be able to enjoy a meal when you can eat whatever you like without worrying about whether the foods are allowed or not. Please note that this means two meals a week and not two days a week. But take note! You are not allowed second helpings of the same dish — for everything you eat and drink, you can have one 'unit' only. Make sure that you space these meals out to give your body time to recover.

ONE DAY OF PURE PROTEINS (PP) PER WEEK

This day of pure proteins will guarantee that you do not put any weight back on. So you will be allowed only the Attack phase proteins (see the list on page 11), with no limit on quantity. Make this little effort, because it is the only restriction in the Consolidation phase. As far as you possibly can, keep Thursdays as your pure protein day and avoid all 'tolerated foods' (see the list on page 13).

WHAT CAN I EAT DURING CONSOLIDATION?

You can eat all the foods from the Attack phase and the Cruise phase on pages 11 and 13, and you are also now allowed foods from the tolerated list on page 13 (except during Protein Thursdays).

STARCHY FOODS
(1–2 SERVINGS PER WEEK)

Bulgur wheat
Couscous
Dried peas
Flageolet beans
Garden peas
Haricot beans
Kidney beans
Lentils
Pasta (preferably wholemeal)
Polenta
Rice (preferably brown or wild)
Split peas

BREAD
(2 SLICES PER DAY)

Brown bead
Wholemeal bread

CHEESE
(1 PORTION PER DAY)

Cheddar
Comté
Edam
Emmental
Gouda

FRUIT
(1–2 PORTIONS PER DAY)

ALL EXCEPT:
Bananas
Cherries
Dried fruit and nuts
Grapes

MEAT
(IN ADDITION TO MEATS ON THE ATTACK & CRUISE LISTS)

Leg of lamb
Roast pork fillet

PHASE 4: STABILIZATION

Stabilization comes with three simple, concrete but non-negotiable measures.

A PROTEIN THURSDAY EVERY WEEK

From now on you are free to eat normally six days out of seven, but this final permanent instruction will be all there is to protect you from your tendency to put weight back on. On this day, you will select the purest possible proteins. You may also on occasion use powdered proteins (but not just any old powder) if this can help you.

As with the Consolidation phase, this instruction is of course non-negotiable — you must persevere with the habit you acquired during your diet.

3 TABLESPOONS OF OAT BRAN PER DAY

Eating oat bran every day is beneficial for your health and will help to ensure that your newly rediscovered figure is there for good.

A MAJOR CONTRACT — YOU AGREE TO GIVE UP LIFTS AND ESCALATORS

If you are not sporty, give up taking lifts and escalators and avoid using your car for very short journeys: in other words, get yourself moving! To motivate yourself, you can buy a pedometer to count the number of steps you take each day. You don't have to turn into a top-level athlete, but part of your daily routine is to get your legs working. You will be looking after the planet as well as your health!

WALK

Walk for at least 20 minutes every day.

WHAT CAN I EAT DURING STABILIZATION?

Except for one day a week, anything you want!

Thursdays are strictly protein-only. Use the purest possible protein foods (see the Attack list on page 11).

On your protein Thursdays, you are not allowed 'tolerated' foods (please refer to the list on page 13).

TOP 10 ATTACK

SMOKED SALMON
WITH CHIVE SCRAMBLED EGG

Serves 2 Preparation time: 5 minutes Cooking time: 5-6 minutes

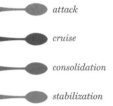

attack

cruise

consolidation

stabilization

A great idea for a breakfast dish if you're looking for a substitute for cereals and toast. If you don't like fish, you can serve the chive scrambled egg with shredded cooked chicken or just on its own for breakfast, lunch or dinner.

4 eggs
1 tbsp fat-free fromage frais
Seasoning
2 tsp chopped fresh chives
60g smoked salmon, cut into strips

Whisk the eggs and fromage frais together with seasoning.

Heat a non-stick pan and pour in the egg mixture. Cook for a minute and then, using a spatula, gently push the egg around to allow it all to cook.

When the egg looks like creamy curds, stir in the chives and smoked salmon and serve immediately.

Once you reach the Cruise phase, serve with grilled tomatoes, mushrooms or asparagus for a delicious light brunch.

CRISPY COD
WITH LEMON SAUCE

Serves 4 Preparation time: **20 minutes** Cooking time: **10–15 minutes**

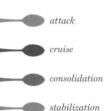

attack

cruise

consolidation

stabilization

Oat bran is an essential part of the Dukan diet, so this recipe is a great way of making sure you get the 1½ tablespoons you need each day in the Attack phase. Cod is used in this recipe, but other white fish such as haddock could be substituted, as could salmon. Vary the herbs too — dill and parsley are a great combination with salmon. This is delicious served with new potatoes if you're not following the Dukan diet.

1 tbsp chopped fresh parsley
1 tbsp chopped fresh chives
6 tbsp oat bran
Grated zest of 2 lemons
1 egg, beaten
4 x 200g cod fillets

3 tbsp fat-free fromage frais
3 tbsp virtually fat-free cottage cheese
1–2 tbsp skimmed milk
Few drops of lemon juice
Black pepper

Preheat the oven to 180°C/350°F/Gas 4.

Mix together the herbs, oat bran and lemon zest and place on a plate.

Place the beaten egg in a shallow bowl.

Dip the cod fillets in the egg, then roll in the herb/oat bran mixture, and then place on a baking sheet. Bake in the oven for 10–15 minutes until the fish is cooked through.

Meanwhile, place the fromage frais, cottage cheese, skimmed milk, lemon juice and black pepper in a small blender and blend until smooth. Pour into a small pan and heat gently to serve spooned over the fish.

LEMON GRASS & GINGER MUSSELS

Serves 4 Preparation time: 15 minutes Cooking time: 7 minutes

I love mussels and they're great for the Attack phase of the diet when you can add lots of different flavours. And, of course, anyone not following the Dukan can enjoy them with crusty bread. Clean mussels by soaking them first in cold water, then scrubbing with a small brush, pulling off any barnacles or 'beards'. Do not cook any mussels that are already open and discard any that do not open during cooking.

attack

cruise

consolidation

stabilization

1 stalk lemon grass, sliced
1 garlic clove, peeled and diced
2cm piece fresh root ginger, peeled and diced
1 red chilli, deseeded and diced

2–3 kaffir lime leaves
2kg mussels, de-bearded and cleaned
2 tbsp chopped fresh coriander leaves

Pour 200ml water into a large pan or wok and add the lemon grass, garlic, ginger, chilli and lime leaves. Bring to the boil and then reduce the heat.

Add the mussels, stir them and cover the pan tightly with a lid. Cook for 3–4 minutes.

Remove the lid to check all the mussels have opened. If they have not, return the lid and cook for a further 1–2 minutes.

Spoon the mussels into warmed dishes and spoon over the liquid.

Sprinkle with chopped coriander leaves to serve.

Once you are in the Cruise phase, these are delicious served over a bowl of steamed pak choi.

BACON-WRAPPED SCALLOPS

Serves 4 Preparation time: 10 minutes Cooking time: 15–18 minutes

Delicious little morsels of seafood and bacon flavoured with tarragon — perfect for the Attack phase, but also a great little starter if you are inviting friends over for dinner. Other herbs that work well in this recipe include parsley or chives. Scallops are easily cleaned by washing under cold water and it's a personal choice as to whether you eat the coral (roe) part or not — I think its creaminess and flavour are worth it!

12 scallops, cleaned
2 tsp chopped fresh tarragon
6 rashers light bacon, halved lengthways

Preheat the oven to 200°C/400°F/Gas 6.

Roll the scallops in the chopped tarragon to coat lightly with the herb.

Wrap each scallop in half a bacon rasher. Place on a baking sheet and bake in the oven for 15–18 minutes.

Serve warm.

attack

cruise

consolidation

stabilization

SEAFOOD KEBABS

Serves 4 Preparation time: 10 minutes + 20 minutes marinating   Cooking time: 8–10 minutes

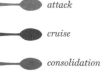

attack

cruise

consolidation

stabilization

Kebabs are a perfect summer dish that all the family can enjoy, so these would be a great Dukan addition to your normal weekend barbecue. They are also great served with a dipping sauce of fat-free yoghurt, lemon juice and chopped herbs.

1 garlic clove, peeled and crushed
1 tbsp grated fresh root ginger
1 tsp chilli flakes
2 tsp tomato purée
2 tbsp lemon juice
1 tsp soy sauce

400g large raw prawns
150g scallops, cleaned
200g monkfish, skinless,
   cut into large chunks
1 tbsp chopped fresh parsley

Mix together the garlic, ginger, chilli flakes, tomato purée, lemon juice and soy sauce.

Place the seafood and monkfish in a non-metallic bowl and pour over the marinade. Rub into the seafood and fish and then leave to stand for 20 minutes.

Thread the seafood and fish onto wooden kebab sticks that have been soaked in water for 15 minutes to prevent them from burning. Cook the kebabs for 4–5 minutes on each side, either under a hot grill or on a barbecue, basting with any remaining marinade, until cooked. Be careful not to overcook.

Serve immediately sprinkled with chopped parsley.

Once you reach the Cruise phase, you can thread chopped red peppers, cherry tomatoes and courgettes on to the kebab sticks to add colour and texture. Serve on a bed of salad leaves for a really substantial, tasty meal that the whole family can enjoy.

HERB TURKEY ESCALOPES

Serves 4 Preparation time: **15 minutes** Cooking time: **8-12 minutes**

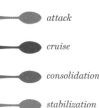

attack

cruise

consolidation

stabilization

This recipe can also be made with chicken, if you prefer. The herby crust provides your daily intake of oat bran for the Attack phase and you can choose your favourite herbs for the crust too.

4 x 150g turkey steaks
2 eggs, beaten
6 tbsp oat bran
4 tbsp chopped fresh basil
Seasoning

Preheat the oven to 200°C/400°F/Gas 6. Place the turkey steaks between two sheets of cling film and use a rolling pin to flatten out to thin escalopes.

Place the egg in a shallow bowl. Mix together the oat bran, basil and seasoning and place on a flat plate. Dip each turkey escalope into the egg, and then into the oat bran mixture to coat.

Heat 3 drops of oil in a non-stick frying pan and wipe off with kitchen paper. Cook the turkey for 3–4 minutes on each side.

Transfer to the oven for 2–3 minutes, or until the turkey is cooked through.

Once you get to the Cruise phase, serve with steamed vegetables or a leafy green salad.

PEPPERED STEAK
WITH HORSERADISH SAUCE

Serves 1 Preparation time: **10 minutes** Cooking time: **8 minutes**

Treating yourself to lots of steak is one of the best things about the Attack phase! Choose lean steak, cutting off any excess fat before you cook, and always leave your steak to rest at room temperature before cooking, and again after cooking, to ensure optimum tenderness. If you wish, you could also cook the steak over a barbecue.

attack

cruise

consolidation

stabilization

1 tbsp fat-free fromage frais
25g tofu
1 tsp horseradish sauce
2 tsp chopped fresh parsley
Seasoning
1 tbsp black peppercorns, crushed
200–250g fillet steak

To make the horseradish sauce, place the fromage frais, tofu and horseradish in a small blender and blend until smooth. Loosen with a little water if needed. Stir in the chopped parsley and season to taste.

For the steak, place the crushed peppercorns onto a plate and press the steak into the peppercorns on both sides.

Heat a griddle pan until smoking hot, add the steak and griddle for 3–4 minutes on each side, or until cooked to your liking. Set aside for 5 minutes before serving.

Serve the steak with a dollop of horseradish sauce on the side.

When you reach the Cruise phase, this steak is great served with a leafy green salad.

THAI BEEF SOUP

Serves 4 Preparation time: **10 minutes** Cooking time: **10 minutes**

If you like, you can substitute the beef with prawns or chunks of white fish. I find this is a great dish for a cold winter's evening, when you want something warming and spicy, but not stodgy and unhealthy.

900ml vegetable stock
4 spring onions, sliced
1 red chilli, deseeded and diced
1cm piece fresh root ginger,
   peeled and diced

200g beef fillet, cut into thin strips
1 tsp soy sauce
2 tbsp chopped fresh coriander

attack
cruise
consolidation
stabilization

Place the stock in a pan with the spring onions, chilli and ginger and bring to the boil.

Add the beef and simmer for 5–6 minutes, until the beef is cooked.

Stir in the soy sauce to taste and serve sprinkled with the chopped coriander.

✗ ·

Once you have reached the Cruise phase, this recipe is delicious made with the addition of roughly chopped Chinese cabbage and bean sprouts.

· ·

SPICY EGG-TOPPED BURGER
WITH MUSTARD SAUCE

Serves 4 Preparation time: 12 minutes + 15-20 minutes chilling Cooking time: 25-30 minutes

attack

cruise

consolidation

stabilization

Everyone loves a burger, and just because you are on a diet, doesn't mean you have to go without! Adding spices and herbs to the mince really brings out the meaty flavour, and these are perfect for serving to the rest of the family with burger buns if they wish.

550g minced beef
1 onion, peeled and finely diced
½ tsp chilli powder
½ tbsp Dijon mustard
1 tbsp chopped fresh coriander
5 eggs

For the mustard sauce
150g fat-free quark
100ml skimmed milk
½ tsp Dijon mustard
Seasoning

To make the burgers, place the minced beef, onion, chilli powder, mustard and half the chopped coriander in a large bowl. Beat 1 of the eggs, add to the bowl and mix everything together well (using your hands works best, squeezing the ingredients together). With wet hands, shape the mixture into four burgers, then place in the fridge to chill for 15–20 minutes.

Heat the grill and cook the burgers for 12–15 minutes on each side, until cooked through.

To make the mustard sauce, whisk together the light cream cheese, skimmed milk, mustard and seasoning in a small pan over a gentle heat until smooth and creamy.

Meanwhile, bring a frying pan of water to a simmer and gently drop in the remaining eggs. Poach for 5–6 minutes (depending on how well done you like your eggs), then remove with a slotted spoon.

Serve the burgers topped with the poached eggs and with a spoonful of sauce poured over. Sprinkle with the remaining chopped coriander to serve.

✕ •

If you are in the Cruise phase, serve these with a crisp green salad on the side.

• •

SWEET SOUFFLÉ OMELETTE

Serves 1 Preparation time: **12 minutes** Cooking time: **20–25 minutes**

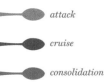

attack

cruise

consolidation

stabilization

If you love eggs for breakfast, but are getting fed up with boiled or poached, try this delicious sweet omelette. Orange water is perfect for adding that little extra flavour.

2 eggs
1 tbsp fat-free natural yoghurt
½–¾ tsp sweetener
2 drops orange flower water (optional)
Large pinch of ground cinnamon
Pinch of grated nutmeg

Separate the eggs and place the whites in a large grease-free bowl. Whisk until soft peaks form. Fold in the egg yolks, yoghurt, sweetener, orange flower water (if using) and cinnamon.

Heat 3 drops of oil in a non-stick frying pan over a medium heat and wipe off with kitchen paper. Pour in the omelette mixture. Move around a little to cook all the egg, and then leave to cook for a minute to set.

Fold the omelette in half and slide onto a plate. Sprinkle with the grated nutmeg to serve.

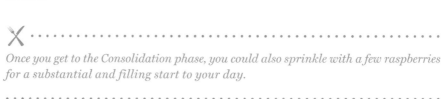

Once you get to the Consolidation phase, you could also sprinkle with a few raspberries for a substantial and filling start to your day.

LUNCH BOX

MINI PRAWN & DILL QUICHES

Makes 12 Preparation time: **15 minutes** Cooking time: **15–18 minutes**

These individual quiches are perfect for lunch boxes or picnics. I find they make a really tasty alternative to the pastry version and you can start enjoying them as early as the Cruise phase.

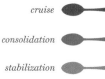

cruise

consolidation

stabilization

4 large eggs and 2 large egg yolks
150ml low-fat crème fraîche
Seasoning
1½ tbsp chopped fresh dill
12 raw king prawns
50g reduced-fat Emmental cheese, grated

Preheat the oven to 190°C/375°F/Gas 5. Line a 12-hole muffin tin with paper muffin cases or squares of greaseproof paper or just lightly oil the tin by wiping with 3 drops of oil and some kitchen paper.

In a bowl, whisk together the whole eggs, egg yolks, crème fraîche, seasoning and dill. Transfer to a jug for ease of pouring.

Place a prawn in the bottom of each muffin case, then pour over the egg mixture.

Sprinkle each one with the grated cheese, then bake in the oven for 15–18 minutes until the tops are golden.

✗ ·

Vary the fillings depending on what you have — chunks of salmon or crispy low-fat bacon in the Attack and Cruise PP phases or peppers and roast vegetables in the Cruise PV phase — the list is endless.

· ·

SPICED BUTTERNUT WEDGES
WITH BUTTER BEAN DIP

Serves 4 Preparation time: **15 minutes** Cooking time: **30-35 minutes**

consolidation

stabilization

If pumpkins are in season, this recipe works well with those too, and I think roasting really brings out their nutty flavour and is so simple! Most canned beans can also be used to make creamy, filling dips in this way – just add the spices or herbs of your choice.

800g butternut squash or pumpkin,
   peeled (if pumpkin), deseeded and
   cut into thick wedges
1 tsp olive oil
1 tsp cumin seeds
6–8 fresh sage leaves, chopped
Seasoning

400g tin butter beans, drained
2 garlic cloves, peeled
Juice of 1 lemon
50g extra-light cream cheese
1 tsp ground cumin
1 tsp paprika

Preheat the oven to 190°C/375°F/Gas 5.

Place the butternut wedges in a roasting tray and sprinkle with the olive oil, the cumin seeds and sage, season well and roast in the oven for 30–35 minutes, tossing occasionally, until tender.

Meanwhile, blend together the butter beans, garlic, lemon juice, cream cheese, ground cumin, paprika and seasoning. Add a little water to loosen if needed.

Serve the wedges on a platter with a dish of the dip in the middle so everyone can help themselves. To make a perfect take-away lunch, pack the wedges in one container and the dip in another.

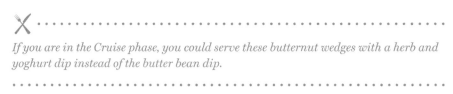

If you are in the Cruise phase, you could serve these butternut wedges with a herb and yoghurt dip instead of the butter bean dip.

TUNA &
BEAN SALAD

Serves 4 Preparation time: 15 minutes

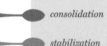

consolidation

stabilization

I change the beans in this salad depending on what is in my store cupboard, so don't be too precious about following the recipe to the letter. Just check what you are allowed — watercress could be changed for rocket or other salad leaves.

400g tin butter beans, drained
200g tin tuna in spring water, drained
1 small red onion, peeled and thinly sliced
1 red pepper, deseeded and thinly sliced
Small handful of fresh parsley,
   roughly chopped

12 cherry tomatoes, halved
75g watercress
1 tsp olive oil
1 tsp red wine vinegar
½ tsp Dijon mustard
Seasoning

Place the beans in a large bowl and flake in the tuna.

Add the onion, pepper, parsley and cherry tomatoes and toss together gently.

Place the watercress on a large platter and spoon over the tuna salad.

Mix together the olive oil, wine vinegar and mustard with some seasoning
and pour over the salad to serve.

CHEESE & ONION FLATBREAD
WITH HOUMOUS

Serves 2 Preparation time: **15 minutes** Cooking time: **8-10 minutes**

 *consolidation*

stabilization

This is a quick recipe that I make if I know I'm going to be out and about for the day as it can easily be packed up in a lunch box for a take-away lunch or tasty snack. The recipe also provides half your daily intake of oat bran for the Stabilization phase. For a herb flatbread, just stir in a tablespoon of chopped parsley or chives before cooking.

For the flatbread
4 tbsp oat bran
3 tbsp fat-free natural yoghurt
1 egg, beaten
2 spring onions, finely chopped
25g Cheddar cheese, grated

For the houmous
400g tin chickpeas, drained and rinsed
1 garlic clove, peeled
2 tbsp fat-free natural yoghurt
Small handful of fresh parsley
Juice of ½ lemon
Pinch of paprika
Seasoning

To make the flatbread, mix together the oat bran, yoghurt, egg, spring onions and grated cheese.

Heat 3 drops of oil in a non-stick frying pan over a medium heat and wipe off with kitchen paper. Spread the mixture around the pan, making a flat surface.

Cook for 4–5 minutes until the underneath is golden. Gently turn over and cook for a further 4–5 minutes, then remove from the pan and cut into wedges.

For the houmous, place everything in a blender and blend until nearly smooth. If you want a looser texture, just add a little water.

Serve the houmous on wedges of the cheesy bread with salad, if wished.

SCOTCH EGGS

Serves 4 Preparation time: **15 minutes** Cooking time: **35 minutes**

Everyone loves Scotch eggs and these are far healthier than shop-bought ones, plus you can add your own choice of spices and herbs to the sausage mixture if you wish. Delicious for taking on picnics or for a lunch box for work, this recipe is really simple to make and will be enjoyed by the whole family.

consolidation
stabilization

5 large eggs
8 low-fat sausages
2 slices wholemeal bread, made into crumbs
1 tbsp oat bran
Salad, to serve

Preheat the oven to 190°C/375°F/Gas 5. Cook 4 of the eggs in boiling water for 8 minutes. Remove from the pan and refresh under cold running water. Leave to cool slightly to make them easier to handle, then peel away the shells.

Remove the skin from the sausages and, using the meat from 2 sausages for each hard-boiled egg, make the sausage meat into a ball in your hand and then press the egg into it, gradually working around the whole egg to seal it in completely.

Beat the remaining egg and place in a shallow bowl. Mix together the breadcrumbs and oat bran and place on a plate or chopping board.

Coat the covered eggs in beaten egg, then roll in the breadcrumb mix to coat completely. Place on a baking tray and cook in the oven for 20–25 minutes until golden.

Serve with a summer salad.

 . . . .

Refreshing hard-boiled eggs under cold water at the end of the cooking time stops the cooking process and prevents the eggs having a circle of grey around the yolk when you open them up.

. . . .

SPINACH, BROAD BEAN & FETA SALAD

Serves 4 Preparation time: 15 minutes Cooking time: 15 minutes

stabilization

Quinoa is a great ingredient that can be used instead of couscous or bulgur wheat in any recipe and it is higher in protein. You don't have to remove the outer skin of the broad beans, but sometimes they can be quite tough, so it is worth the effort!

200g quinoa
300g broad beans (podded weight)
200g baby spinach leaves
2 tbsp chopped fresh mint
200g feta cheese, crumbled
50g black olives, stoned and halved

1 tsp olive oil
Juice of ½ lemon
½ tsp harissa paste
30g pecan nuts, toasted and
  roughly chopped

Place the quinoa in a pan, cover with boiling water and simmer for 8–10 minutes until cooked. Drain in a sieve and refresh under cold water.

Meanwhile cook the broad beans in simmering water for 12–15 minutes until tender. Drain and rinse under cold water, then take off the outer skin of the each bean.

Place the beans in a large bowl with the quinoa, spinach, mint, feta cheese and olives.

Whisk together the olive oil, lemon juice and harissa paste and stir into the quinoa salad.

Serve sprinkled with toasted pecan nuts.

VEGETABLE SPRING ROLLS

Serves 2 Preparation time: 15 minutes Cooking time: 6–8 minutes

cruise pv

consolidation

stabilization

These delicate little spring rolls provide a perfect lunch and I often make them if I want something hot for lunchtime instead of a salad, but still healthy. You can vary the filling to include prawns or cooked chicken and they also make a lovely light starter.

1 large courgette
5g bean sprouts
1 carrot, peeled and cut into matchsticks
¼ red pepper, deseeded and cut into matchsticks
2 spring onions, shredded
4–6 fresh mint leaves
4–6 fresh coriander leaves
Seasoning

Thinly slice the courgette using a vegetable peeler and place the strips on a work surface.

Mix together the remaining ingredients. Place a small amount of the vegetable mixture at the end of each strip of courgette, and then roll to encase the vegetables.

Place in a steamer and steam for 6–8 minutes, until the vegetables are tender. The rolls can be served warm or allowed to cool for a packed lunch.

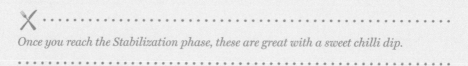

Once you reach the Stabilization phase, these are great with a sweet chilli dip.

SALMON BLINIS

Makes 12 Preparation time: **5 minutes** Cooking time: **12-15 minutes**

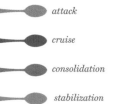

attack

cruise

consolidation

stabilization

Blinis are a fantastic find for the Attack phase of the diet. You can top these little blinis with any fish of your choice. Smoked trout or salmon are the most traditional, but if you can find smoked eel, that also works really well.

6 tbsp oat bran
70g fat-free natural yoghurt
2 eggs, beaten
Pinch of wasabi powder
Pinch of black pepper
3–4 tbsp fat-free fromage frais
125g smoked salmon, cut into strips
2 tbsp snipped fresh chives

Mix together the oat bran, yoghurt, eggs, wasabi powder and pepper.

Heat 3 drops of oil in a non-stick frying pan over a medium heat and wipe off with kitchen paper. Drop a few small spoonfuls of the batter into the pan. Cook for 2–3 minutes until bubbles start to appear, then turn over and cook for a further 1–2 minutes, until golden. Remove from the frying pan.

Repeat with the remaining batter.

Top the blinis with a dollop of fat-free fromage frais, a swirl of smoked salmon and a sprinkling of chives and serve immediately. If you are making a packed lunch, it is easy to take all the components in separate containers.

CARROT & ORANGE PÂTÉ

Serves 4-6 Preparation time: **20 minutes + 1 hour chilling** Cooking time: **12-18 minutes**

An unusual pâté, without meat for a change, and very healthy. Perfect for any vegetarians in your family and to make sure you're getting your five-a-day too!

consolidation

stabilization

1 small onion, peeled and diced
225g carrots, peeled and thinly sliced
Zest and juice of 1 orange
Seasoning
¼ tsp ground cumin

2 tbsp fat-free fromage frais
½ tsp Dijon mustard
1 tbsp chopped fresh parsley
Vegetable crudités, to serve

Heat 3 drops of oil in a large non-stick pan and wipe off with kitchen paper. Sauté the onion for 4–5 minutes until softened.

Add the carrot, orange zest and juice, seasoning, ground cumin and 200ml water. Bring to the boil, cover and simmer for 6–8 minutes, until the carrot is tender. Remove the lid and increase the heat to cook until all the liquid has evaporated.

Remove from the heat and leave to cool for 10 minutes. Pour into a food processor and blend until smooth. Add the fromage frais and mustard and blend again.

Stir in the chopped parsley and then spoon into ramekins or small bowls. Cover and chill for at least 1 hour before serving with vegetable crudités.

You can add 2 chopped apricots to the carrots when cooking to give a thicker texture and additional flavour.

EGG & VEGETABLE FRIED RICE

Serves 4 Preparation time: 15 minutes Cooking time: 15 minutes

Fried rice is such a treat, and this can be eaten on its own as a meal or as a side dish with other recipes such as Seafood Kebabs (page 28) or Creamy Herb-stuffed Chicken Breast (page 89). Leftovers of this recipe are perfect to take to the office in a Tupperware container.

consolidation

stabilization

200g brown rice
1 red chilli, deseeded and finely diced
3 garlic cloves, peeled and crushed
3 eggs, beaten
2 large carrots, peeled and diced

200g Chinese cabbage, shredded
4 spring onions, sliced
200g peas or soya beans, fresh or frozen
2 tsp soy sauce

Cook the rice in boiling water according to the pack instructions. Drain.

In a small blender, blend together the chilli and garlic to a paste.

Heat 3 drops of oil in a wok or large non-stick frying pan and wipe off with kitchen paper. Add the eggs, stirring constantly until they are cooked. Turn out onto a board and roughly chop.

Again, heat 3 drops of oil in the wok or frying pan and wipe off with kitchen paper. Cook the carrots for 4–5 minutes. Stir in the cabbage and chilli paste and continue to cook for another minute. Add the rice and stir-fry for another minute before adding the cooked egg, the spring onions, peas and soy sauce, then continue to cook until everything is heated through. Serve hot or cold.

In the Cruise phase in particular you could replace the brown rice with konjac rice which is very low in calories, carbohydrates and sugar. You can find it in health food shops.

SWEETCORN & ONION FRITTERS

Makes 8 Preparation time: **6 minutes** Cooking time: **16-20 minutes**

consolidation

stabilization

Another great recipe that includes oat bran, these fritters are perfect for packing up for a lunchtime snack. Instead of the tomato sauce, serve topped with wafer-thin ham or low-fat cottage cheese and a sprinkling of paprika for a bit of a kick.

2 eggs
3 tbsp oat bran
1 tsp baking powder
125g sweetcorn kernels
2 spring onions, thinly sliced
2 tsp chopped fresh parsley or chives
Seasoning
Tomato salsa (see page 94), to serve (optional)

Whisk the eggs with the oat bran and baking powder, then stir in the sweetcorn, spring onions, herbs and seasoning.

Heat 3 drops of oil in a non-stick frying pan over a medium heat and wipe off with kitchen paper. Drop three or four individual tablespoons of the mixture into the pan. Cook for 4–5 minutes until golden and then carefully turn over and cook for another 4–5 minutes on the other side.

Remove from the pan, place on kitchen paper and keep warm whilst you cook the remaining fritters.

Serve with tomato salsa if wished.

HARICOT BEAN, TUNA & MINT PÂTÉ

Serves 4 Preparation time: **10 minutes**

A really clever kind of dip or pâté that you can bulk up with lots of crudités, this is a super-quick and simple starter or snack to take to work in your lunch box. If you don't have a food processor, use a fork or potato masher — you will just have a slightly chunkier pâté.

consolidation

stabilization

400g tin haricot beans,
   drained and rinsed
Juice of ½ lemon
1 tbsp fat-free Greek yoghurt
Seasoning

130g tin tuna in spring water,
   drained
1 tbsp chopped fresh mint
Red and yellow peppers,
   deseeded and sliced, to serve

Place the drained haricot beans, lemon juice, yoghurt and seasoning in a food processor. Add half of the tinned tuna and process until nearly smooth.

Spoon into a bowl and stir in the remaining tuna and the chopped mint.

Serve with sliced peppers for dipping.

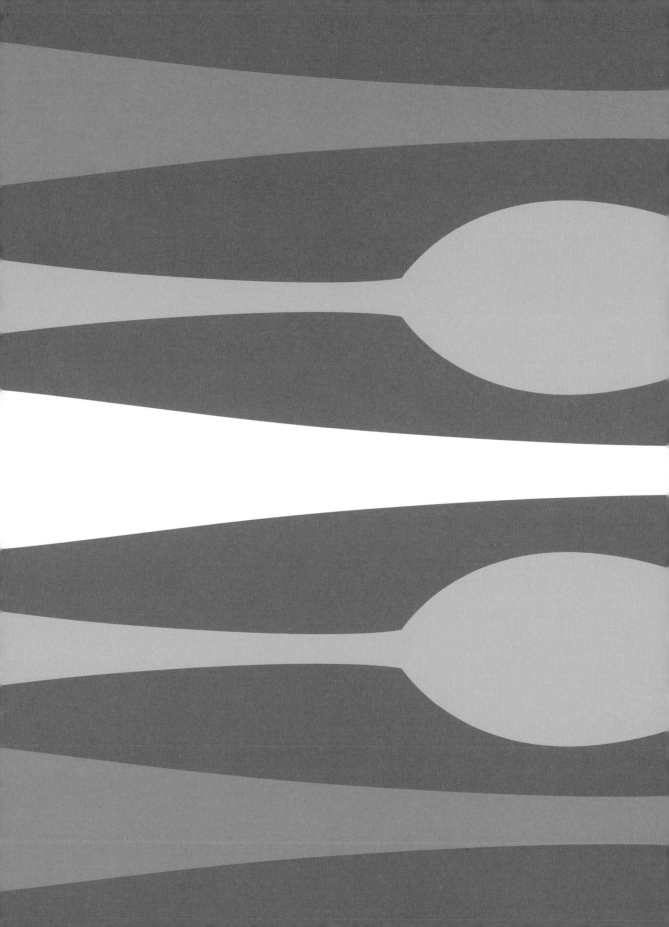

SOUPS, SNACKS & STARTERS

SPICY SALMON BROTH

Makes 4 Preparation time: 15 minutes Cooking time: 20 minutes

The base for this broth could be used for other soups too — try with chicken, turkey or prawns. The addition of rice in the Consolidation phase turns this soup into something much more substantial. If you want a little more heat, just add another chilli.

cruise pv

consolidation

stabilization

2 red chillies, deseeded and thinly sliced
1 stalk lemon grass, thinly sliced
1 tsp grated fresh root ginger
1 garlic clove, peeled and crushed
1.5 litres fish or vegetable stock
Juice of ½ lime
2 tsp soy sauce
6 baby carrots, peeled and sliced

40g bean sprouts
4 spring onions, chopped
2 pak choi, sliced
Small handful of fresh coriander leaves
Small handful of fresh mint leaves
400g salmon fillet, skinned and
  thinly sliced
1 tbsp sesame seeds, to serve (optional)

Heat 3 drops of oil in a non-stick saucepan and wipe off with kitchen paper. Sauté the chillies, lemon grass, ginger and garlic for 1–2 minutes.

Pour in the stock, lime juice and soy sauce, mix well and simmer for 10 minutes. Add the carrots, bean sprouts, spring onions and pak choi and cook for a further 6 minutes.

To serve, divide the coriander, mint and salmon among four bowls, then pour over the hot soup (the heat of the soup will be enough to cook the thinly sliced salmon).

Sprinkle with sesame seeds to serve, if using.

✗ . . . .

If you are in the Consolidation or Stabilization phases, you could add 25g cooked brown rice after the pak choi.

. . . .

CHICKEN & LEEK SOUP

Serves 4 Preparation time: **5 minutes** Cooking time: **25 minutes**

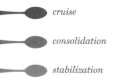

cruise

consolidation

stabilization

A great way to use up leftover chicken, or turkey if you prefer. And if you would like to spice it up, add a little garlic or chilli when searing the leeks. If I don't have any leftover chicken, I just roast a couple of skinless chicken breasts in the oven for 20–25 minutes first.

1 tsp olive oil
4 leeks, washed, trimmed and sliced
500g chicken, cooked and shredded
1 litre chicken stock
Seasoning
Juice of ½ lemon

Heat the oil in a pan over a low heat, then add the leeks and stir around in the oil. Cover the pan and sweat the leeks for 12–15 minutes, stirring occasionally.

Add the chicken, stock, seasoning and lemon juice and cook for a further 10 minutes to allow the flavours to develop and the chicken to warm through. Serve hot.

CORN & BACON CHOWDER

Serves 4 Preparation time: **10 minutes** Cooking time: **20 minutes**

This soup is perfect for a cold winter's day — chunky and warming, but still healthy.

stabilization

6 rashers light bacon, chopped
1 onion, peeled and finely chopped
1 large potato, peeled and cut into
   1cm cubes
700ml vegetable stock

800ml skimmed milk
400g sweetcorn kernels, frozen and
   defrosted or tinned
Seasoning
3 tbsp snipped fresh chives

Heat 3 drops of oil in a non-stick saucepan and wipe off with kitchen paper. Cook the bacon for 2–3 minutes. Add the onion and potato and cook for a further 2–3 minutes, stirring to prevent the potato from sticking to the pan.

Add the stock and milk, bring to a simmer and cook for 5 minutes, or until the potato is tender.

Stir in the sweetcorn and heat through.

Season and stir in the chives to serve.

. . . .

To make this a Consolidation recipe, you can just omit the potato and replace with butternut squash.

. . . .

CHILLED CUCUMBER & MINT SOUP

Serves 4 Preparation time: **40 minutes** + chilling Cooking time: **5 minutes**

cruise pv

consolidation

stabilization

A great summer soup, perfect to have with Salmon Blinis (page 54) as a light lunch. And on a really hot day, I like to serve it with a couple of ice cubes floating on top.

2 cucumbers
Salt
1 litre vegetable stock
2 spring onions, finely chopped
1 garlic clove, peeled and finely chopped
Small handful of fresh mint
500g fat-free natural yoghurt
Seasoning

Cut the cucumbers in half lengthways. Scoop out the seeds with a small spoon and slice the cucumbers. Place them in a colander and sprinkle with salt, then leave to stand for 20 minutes (this helps to bring out the liquid).

Rinse the sliced cucumber with cold water and pat dry.

Bring the stock to the boil, add the onions and garlic and cook for 2 minutes before adding the cucumber and stalks from the mint. Simmer for 2 minutes, then remove from the heat and take the mint stalks from the soup. Leave to cool for 2–3 minutes.

Blend the soup until smooth, then leave to cool a little more. Blend again with the yoghurt and a few mint leaves. Season to taste. Chill completely.

Serve with a little drizzle of yoghurt and a sprinkling of small mint leaves.

FRENCH ALMOND & ONION SOUP

Serves 4 Preparation time: **15 minutes** Cooking time: **1 hour 20 minutes**

This is a classic onion soup recipe, with the added twist of a small sprinkling of ground almonds that just gives it a creamy texture. The longer you cook the onions, the sweeter the soup becomes, so be patient!

stabilization

600g onions, peeled and thinly sliced
2 garlic cloves, peeled and crushed
½ tsp sweetener
1 litre beef stock
Seasoning
2 tbsp ground almonds
2 tbsp grated reduced-fat Emmental cheese

Heat 3 drops of oil in a large non-stick saucepan and wipe off with kitchen paper. Add the onions, garlic and sweetener and cook, stirring constantly, until the onions start ro turn golden.

Reduce the heat to its lowest setting and leave the onions to cook for 30 minutes.

Pour in the stock and seasoning and scrape the pan well as the onions will have caught a little on the bottom, giving a lovely dark brown caramelized colour and flavour.

Bring to a simmer, cover the pan and cook for 45 minutes.

Serve in warmed bowls, sprinkled with the ground almonds and grated cheese.

✗ ·

If you omit the almonds, this recipe could be eaten in the Consolidation phase.

· ·

GAZPACHO

Serves 4-6 Preparation time: 15 minutes + chilling

This is one of the easiest soups to make, and I think one of the most delicious, especially on a warm summer's day and using lovely fresh produce. The consistency will depend on the ripeness of your ingredients, so add a little water to loosen the soup if needed, and always buy the ripest tomatoes you can find.

1kg ripe tomatoes, roughly chopped
3 garlic cloves, peeled and chopped
4 spring onions, chopped
1 red pepper, deseeded and chopped
4–6 fresh basil leaves

¾ cucumber, chopped
2 tbsp red wine vinegar
Seasoning
3 eggs, hard-boiled,
    shelled and chopped

Place the tomatoes, garlic, spring onions, red pepper, basil and cucumber into a food processor or blender, and blend until finely chopped.

While the machine is still running, slowly pour in the red wine vinegar and a little water.

Season and taste, and then add a little more vinegar or water if you think it needs it. Chill until needed.

Serve in shallow bowls, garnished with chopped eggs.

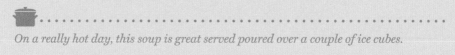

On a really hot day, this soup is great served poured over a couple of ice cubes.

SWEET POTATO & HADDOCK SOUP

Serves 4 **Preparation time: 15 minutes** **Cooking time: 35 minutes**

A really satisfying, warming soup, which you are allowed in the Consolidation phase because the recipe uses sweet potatoes, instead of regular potatoes.

consolidation

stabilization

1 onion, peeled and chopped
350g sweet potatoes, peeled
   and cut into 2cm chunks
1.2 litres fish stock
2 tbsp low-fat crème fraîche

175g smoked haddock,
   cut into bite-size pieces
1 tbsp chopped fresh parsley
Seasoning

Heat 3 drops of oil in a medium non-stick saucepan and wipe off with kitchen paper. Sauté the onion for 4–5 minutes until transparent.

Add the sweet potato and cook for a further 2–3 minutes, stirring occasionally.

Pour in the stock, bring to the boil, and then simmer for 15–18 minutes, until the sweet potato is cooked.

Using a ladle, take out two ladles of soup and blend in a food processor with the crème fraîche until smooth, then return to the pan — this help to thicken the soup.

Add the fish to the pan and continue to cook for 3 minutes, until the fish is cooked through. Sprinkle in the chopped parsley and seasoning to serve.

✕ •

If you want to make this a Cruise phase soup, butternut squash could be used instead of sweet potato.

• •

ENGLISH BREAKFAST TORTILLA

Serves 4-6 Preparation time: **15 minutes** Cooking time: **35 minutes**

All your favourite ingredients in a great-tasting tortilla – hard to believe you are on a diet!

1 onion, peeled and chopped
6 rashers light bacon, chopped
4 low-fat sausages, thickly sliced
8 chestnut mushrooms, quartered

7 eggs
1 tbsp chopped fresh parsley
Seasoning
6 tomatoes, halved

Heat 3 drops of oil in a non-stick frying pan and wipe off with kitchen paper. Sauté the onion for 2–3 minutes before adding the bacon and sausages and cooking for 6–8 minutes. Add the mushrooms and cook for a further 2–3 minutes.

Beat the eggs in a large bowl with the parsley and seasoning, then add the cooked ingredients. Pour the egg mixture back into the frying pan and cook over a medium heat for 15–18 minutes, until golden underneath.

Meanwhile, grill the tomato halves for 4–5 minutes.

Place the frying pan under a hot grill and cook the top of the tortilla for 4–5 minutes until golden.

Turn out onto a chopping board and cut into wedges to serve with the grilled tomatoes.

cruise pv
consolidation
stabilization

SUPERFOOD SALAD

Serves 2 Preparation time: 10 minutes Cooking time: 6-8 minutes

consolidation

stabilization

This salad is really filling and has so many wonderful flavours, and if you like other vegetables, just add them to the mix! If you can't find alfalfa sprouts, any other sprouted seeds or legumes will be just as delicious.

2 smoked mackerel fillets
75g broccoli florets
Small handful of baby spinach leaves
4 radishes, sliced
6 cherry tomatoes, halved
1 red pepper, deseeded and sliced

25g tinned chickpeas
Small handful of alfalfa sprouts
½ tsp Dijon mustard
1 tsp white wine vinegar
1 tsp vegetable oil

Heat the mackerel fillets according to the pack instructions.

Steam or blanch the broccoli in boiling water, then refresh under cold running water. Drain.

Toss together the broccoli, spinach leaves, radishes, tomatoes, pepper, chickpeas and sprouts.

Break up the mackerel fillets and add to the salad.

Mix together the mustard, white wine vinegar and oil and use to dress the salad. Serve immediately.

 . . . .

Turning your own alfalfa seeds into sprouts is really easy — just soak in water overnight and drain, then refresh with water every day until they sprout.

. . . .

EGG, HAM & BEAN SALAD

Serves 4 Preparation time: **12 minutes** Cooking time: **10 minutes**

A quick but delicious salad that you can eat with all the family. Perfect when you have little time to spare, but hungry mouths waiting to be fed! Great with new potatoes or baked potatoes for anyone not on Dukan.

consolidation

stabilization

4 eggs
250g green beans
400g tin butter beans, drained and rinsed
1 cos lettuce, leaves roughly torn
25g rocket leaves

175g lean ham, shredded
Juice of ½ lemon
2 tsp smooth mustard
1 tsp olive oil

Cook the eggs in boiling water for 6–8 minutes, until hard-boiled. Refresh under running cold water, then peel and cut into quarters.

Blanch the green beans in boiling water for 2–3 minutes, refresh under running cold water, then drain.

Gently toss together the green beans, butter beans, lettuce, rocket, ham and eggs.

Whisk together the remaining ingredients and pour over the salad to serve.

SMOKY AUBERGINE & CORIANDER DIP
WITH CRUDITÉS

Serves 6 Preparation time: **12 minutes** Cooking time: **20–25 minutes**

cruise

consolidation

stabilization

A great party dish or perfect for a lunch box or picnic. If you are making this dip in the summer, you can cook the aubergines on a barbecue. Just cook them until they are black and then peel off the skin to reveal the creamy flesh. This also gives a great flavour to the dip.

4 aubergines
1 tsp cumin seeds
1 tsp coriander seeds
1 tsp garam masala
1 red chilli, deseeded and diced
1 garlic clove, peeled and crushed

Juice of 1 lime
Seasoning
1 tbsp chopped fresh coriander
2–3 tbsp fat-free natural yoghurt
Crudités (such as carrots, celery and
    peppers, cut into batons), to serve

Preheat the oven to 200°C/400°F/Gas 6.

Place the aubergines in a roasting tray and roast in the oven for 20–25 minutes, or until softened. Leave to cool, then peel.

Toast the cumin and coriander seeds in a frying pan over a low heat — they are ready when you can smell their wonderful fragrance. Transfer to a pestle and mortar and grind to a powder.

In a food processor, blend together all the spices, the cooked aubergines, chilli, garlic and lime juice.

Season to taste, then stir in the chopped coriander and enough yoghurt to loosen the dip.

Serve with a selection of crudités.

 . . . .

Aubergines can also be cooked on an open flame, either a gas hob or barbecue — just keep turning them until the skin is all black.

. . . .

PRAWNS
WITH A SPICY DIP

Serves 4 Preparation time: 10 minutes

An easy and quick starter that I think you'll really enjoy, especially in the Cruise phase. You could also serve this dip with grilled strips of chicken or turkey.

cruise

consolidation

stabilization

200g extra-light cream cheese
100g fat-free natural yoghurt
1 garlic clove, peeled and crushed
2–3 drops lemon juice
¼ tsp chilli flakes
Handful of snipped fresh chives
Seasoning
400g cooked king prawns, peeled

To make the spicy dip, mix together the cream cheese, natural yoghurt, garlic, lemon juice, chilli flakes and chives. Season to taste.

Arrange the prawns on four small plates and serve the dip in a bowl for everyone to share.

✗ ·

If you are on a Cruise PV day, this looks (and tastes!) really nice if you pile the prawns on to little gem lettuce leaves.

· ·

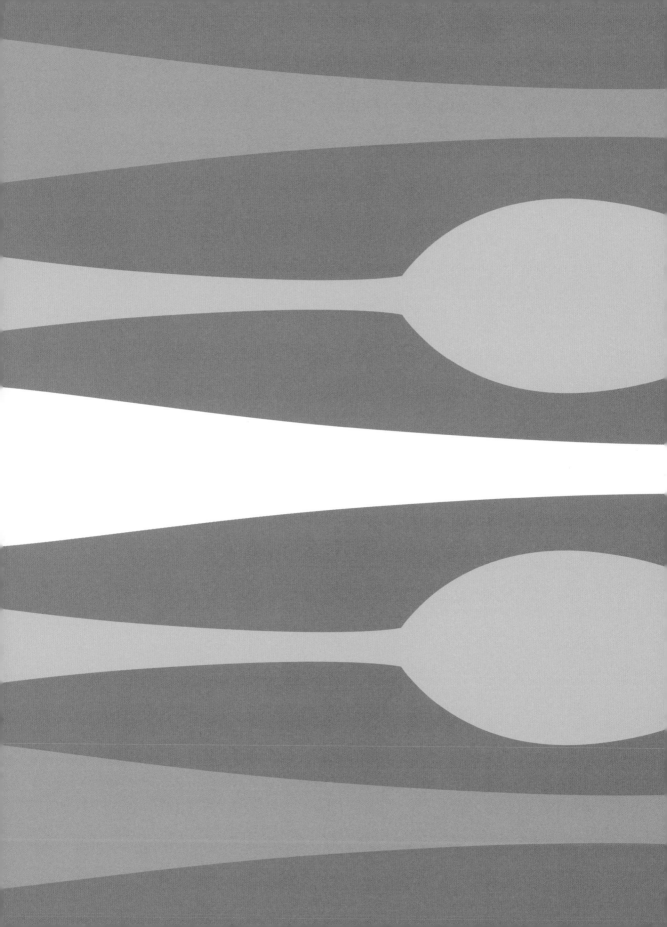

CHICKEN
(& OTHER BIRDS)
TONIGHT

CREAMY HERB-STUFFED CHICKEN BREAST

Serves 4 Preparation time: **20 minutes** Cooking time: **35 minutes**

Stuffing chicken breasts is simple, but adds another flavour and the end result looks impressive, so this is a good standby for when you're cooking for others. Vary your filling depending on the spices and herbs you prefer — tarragon also works really well in this recipe. If you're not following the Dukan diet, this is delicious with mashed potato.

cruise pv

consolidation

stabilization

4 skinless chicken breasts
150g extra-light cream cheese
2 garlic cloves, peeled and crushed
½ tbsp chopped fresh parsley
½ tbsp chopped fresh chives
Seasoning

8 rashers light bacon
2 leeks, washed, trimmed and very
  finely sliced
300g fat-free fromage frais
Crisp green salad leaves, to serve

Preheat the oven to 180°C/350°F/Gas 4.

Make a slit in the side of each chicken breast to create a little pocket.

Mix together the cream cheese, garlic, herbs and seasoning.

Lay a rasher of bacon on a board and place one of the chicken breasts on top. Spoon a quarter of the cream cheese mixture into the pocket of the chicken, and then wrap with the bacon to seal. Repeat with the remaining bacon, cream cheese and chicken.

Place in a roasting tray and bake in the oven for 35 minutes.

Meanwhile, chop the remaining bacon. Heat 3 drops of oil in a non-stick frying pan and wipe off with kitchen paper. Fry the bacon for 1–2 minutes before adding the leeks and stir-frying for 2–3 minutes. Stir in the fromage frais and seasoning.

Remove the chicken breasts from the oven and slice diagonally. Serve on a bed of leeks with the salad leaves.

✕ . . . .

To make this a Cruise PP meal, just omit the leeks and salad leaves.

. . . .

SPICED CHICKEN DRUMSTICKS
WITH TABBOULEH

Serves 4 Preparation time: 30 minutes + marinating Cooking time: 30-35 minutes

consolidation

stabilization

Tabbouleh can be made with couscous, bulgur wheat or quinoa — I just use whatever I have in my store cupboard.

1 tsp vegetable oil
3 garlic cloves, peeled and chopped
2 tbsp grated fresh root ginger
2 tbsp light soy sauce
2 tsp five-spice powder
1kg chicken drumsticks
250g couscous

2 large tomatoes, diced
Large bunch fresh parsley, chopped
Small bunch fresh mint, chopped
1 small red onion, peeled and finely diced
Juice of 1 lemon
Seasoning

Mix together the vegetable oil, garlic, grated ginger, soy sauce and spice powder and place in a non-metallic bowl with the chicken, rubbing it all over the chicken drumsticks. Cover and leave to marinate in the fridge for at least 20–30 minutes, and it could even be left overnight.

Preheat the oven to 180°C/350°F/Gas 4.

Place the chicken drumsticks into a roasting tray and roast in the oven for 30–35 minutes, or until the skin is golden and the chicken is cooked through. You can test this by piercing a drumstick at its thickest part — the juices should run clear.

Meanwhile, to make the tabbouleh, place the couscous in a bowl and just cover with boiling water, then leave to stand for 12–15 minutes until all the liquid has been absorbed.

Fluff up the couscous with a fork, add all the remaining ingredients and mix together well.

Serve the chicken drumsticks on a bed of tabbouleh.

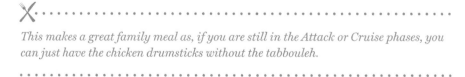

This makes a great family meal as, if you are still in the Attack or Cruise phases, you can just have the chicken drumsticks without the tabbouleh.

CHICKEN KEBABS
WITH WATERCRESS COUSCOUS

Serves 4 Preparation time: 15 minutes + 1 hour marinating Cooking time: 12–14 minutes

You could substitute the chicken for turkey if you prefer. I find kebabs are great for the Attack and Cruise phases of the diet as you can make them with almost any meat, seafood or veggies you have to hand.

consolidation

stabilization

2cm piece fresh root ginger, peeled and chopped
3 garlic cloves, peeled and chopped
Grated zest and juice of 1 orange
4 spring onions, sliced
1 tbsp soy sauce

4 skinless chicken breasts, cut into even-sized cubes
250g couscous
1 mango, stoned, peeled and diced
Seasoning
60g watercress, roughly chopped

Always try to use metal skewers for meat. If you have only bamboo skewers, be sure to soak them well before threading on the ingredients to help prevent them from burning during cooking.

In a pestle and mortar or small blender, blend together the ginger, garlic, orange zest and juice, spring onions and soy sauce. Place the cubed chicken into a non-metallic bowl and pour over the marinade. Leave to marinate in the fridge for 1 hour.

Place the couscous in a bowl and just cover with boiling water, then leave to stand for 12–15 minutes until all the liquid has been absorbed.

Thread the chicken onto eight kebab sticks. Heat a griddle pan until hot and cook the kebabs for 6–7 minutes on each side, until the chicken is cooked through.

Meanwhile, fork through the couscous to break up any lumps, then stir in the mango, seasoning and watercress.

Serve the chicken kebabs on a bed of watercress couscous.

If you are having this as a family meal, but you are in the Attack or Cruise phases, just have the chicken on its own without the watercress couscous.

ORIENTAL
TURKEY BURGERS
WITH TOMATO SALSA

Serves 4 Preparation time: 15 minutes Cooking time: 10-12 minutes

cruise pv

consolidation

stabilization

Turkey meat tends to be leaner than beef and is great for making tasty burgers. I love adding spice to all my food as it gives it so much more flavour and this turkey burger is transformed with the addition of a few Asian spices.

400g minced turkey
2cm piece fresh root ginger,
   peeled and grated
4 spring onions, finely chopped
1 red chilli, deseeded and finely chopped
1 egg yolk

2 tbsp chopped fresh coriander
200g tomatoes, diced
1 small red onion, peeled and finely diced
1 tbsp chopped fresh parsley
1 tbsp red wine vinegar
30g watercress or rocket leaves, to serve

In a large bowl, mix together the minced turkey, ginger, onions, chilli, egg yolk and coriander — this is best done with a fork or even your hands.

Using wet hands, divide the mixture into four and shape into four burgers.

For the salsa, mix together the tomatoes, red onion, parsley and red wine vinegar.

Heat 3 drops of oil in a non-stick frying pan and wipe off with kitchen paper. Cook the burgers for 5–6 minutes on either side, until golden and cooked through.

Serve the burgers on a bed of watercress or rocket, topped with the salsa.

You can have these burgers without the tomato salsa and salad leaves in the Attack phase of the diet.

CHICKEN & BUTTERNUT CASSEROLE

Serves 4 Preparation time: **10 minutes** Cooking time: **35 minutes**

A warming casserole always seems so inviting and un-diet-like! Here, the butternut squash will fill you up and the green beans and mushrooms will increase your vegetable quota.

cruise pv

consolidation

stabilization

400g butternut squash, peeled and diced
1 tsp ground coriander
1 tbsp fresh thyme leaves
1 litre chicken stock
2 garlic cloves, peeled and crushed

Seasoning
4 skinless chicken breasts
200g green beans, trimmed
50g button mushrooms
2 tbsp chopped fresh parsley

Preheat the oven to 190°C/375°F/Gas 5.

Place the butternut, ground coriander, thyme, stock and garlic in a flameproof casserole, season and bring to the boil. Simmer for 10 minutes.

Meanwhile, heat 3 drops of oil in a non-stick frying pan and wipe off with kitchen paper. Brown the chicken breasts all over.

Add the chicken to the casserole, cover and cook in the oven for 15–18 minutes, until the chicken is cooked through.

Remove the chicken breasts and keep warm, and then place the casserole on the hob to boil and reduce the stock for 6–7 minutes. Add the beans and mushrooms, cook for 2–3 minutes, then stir in the chopped parsley to serve, spooned over the chicken breasts.

JERK CHICKEN
WITH RED PEPPER SALSA

Serves 4 Preparation time: **15 minutes + marinating** Cooking time: **25-30 minutes**

If you like your food really spicy and hot, just add another chilli. Using a griddle pan for cooking is brilliant in the early stages of the diet as it gives such a lovely flavour to meat and fish that you don't need lots of accompaniments.

cruise pv

consolidation

stabilization

200g onions, peeled and cut into quarters
1 red chilli, deseeded
3cm piece fresh root ginger, peeled
   and roughly chopped
½ tsp ground allspice
1 tbsp fresh thyme leaves
½ tsp black pepper

100ml white wine vinegar
100ml soy sauce
4 skinless chicken breasts
2 red peppers, deseeded and finely diced
4 spring onions, finely sliced
2 large tomatoes, finely diced
2 tbsp chopped fresh coriander

Place the onions, red chilli, ginger, allspice, thyme leaves, black pepper, wine vinegar and soy sauce in a food processor or blender and blend until smooth.

Place the chicken in a non-metallic bowl and pour over the sauce. Cover and leave to marinate in the fridge for at least 30 minutes or it could be overnight.

Heat a griddle pan until hot and cook the chicken for 25–30 minutes, basting occasionally with the leftover marinade.

Meanwhile, mix together the red peppers, spring onions, tomatoes and coriander for the salsa.

Serve the chicken with the salsa on the side and a green salad if wished.

✗ . . . .

If you are still in the Attack phase, you can have the chicken on its own.

. . . .

TURKEY, BUTTERNUT & SPINACH CURRY

Serves 4-6 Preparation time: **12 minutes** Cooking time: **30 minutes**

cruise pv

consolidation

stabilization

This is a delicious way to make a little meat stretch a long way by adding lots of vegetables. If you want to serve this for a vegetarian, you can omit the turkey and use 200g of tofu instead. Just cut into chunks and add at the end to heat it through. A perfect curry for a night in — no need to call for a take-away any more!

1 small onion, peeled and chopped
1 garlic clove, peeled and chopped
2cm piece fresh root ginger, peeled and chopped
1½ tsp korma spice (hotter curry spice can be used if wished)
Small handful of fresh coriander leaves
300g turkey breast meat, cut into strips

1 red onion, peeled and chopped
450g butternut squash, peeled and chopped into bite-size pieces
150g baby spinach leaves
1 tsp cornflour
1 tsp soy sauce
2 tbsp sweetener
2 tbsp fat-free natural yoghurt

Place the onion, garlic, ginger, korma spice and coriander leaves into a blender and blend until smooth.

Heat this curry paste in a wok or large frying pan and cook the turkey strips and red onion for 2–3 minutes before adding the butternut and 450ml water. Bring to the boil, then simmer for 15–18 minutes, until the butternut is tender.

Stir in the spinach.

Mix together the cornflour, soy sauce, sweetener and 100ml water. Add to the pan and stir until the curry starts to thicken.

Stir in the yoghurt and serve.

 •

If a curry is too hot, serve it with extra yoghurt as this helps to take out the 'heat' of the spice.

• •

SPICED MARINATED CHICKEN BREASTS

Serves 4 Preparation time: **15 minutes** + marinating Cooking time: **10-12 minutes**

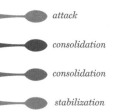

attack

consolidation

consolidation

stabilization

Using a griddle pan to cook meat is a really clever way of helping to reduce the amount of fat consumed as it drains away in the ridges of the pan. For those of you not on the Dukan diet, this goes perfectly with basmati rice.

1 small cinnamon stick
6 cardamom pods
1 tsp cumin seeds
6 whole allspice
1 tsp ground turmeric
1 tsp paprika

4 garlic cloves, peeled and crushed
2cm piece fresh root ginger, peeled
   and chopped
2 tbsp sweetener
1 tsp olive oil
4 skinless chicken breasts

Lightly toast all the spices in a hot dry frying pan. Blitz in a small spice grinder, then tip into a non-metallic bowl.

Using the spice grinder, blitz the garlic and ginger to a paste.

Mix together the spices, ginger and garlic paste, sweetener and olive oil and rub this marinade over the chicken breasts. Leave to marinate in the fridge for 12–24 hours.

Heat a griddle pan until hot and cook the chicken for 4–5 minutes on each side, until cooked through.

If you are on a Cruise PV day, you can serve this spicy chicken with a green salad or any other greens.

CHICKEN KORMA
WITH GREEN PEPPER

Serves 4 Preparation time: **12 minutes** Cooking time: **25 minutes**

This creamy, light curry avoids the unhealthy oils, butter and cream that many curries are loaded with. The curry can be made more 'punchy' by adding a diced red chilli if you like a little more heat. And it's easy to stir your daily oat bran into this recipe too, if you wish.

consolidation

stabilization

1 onion, peeled and roughly chopped
2 garlic cloves, peeled
2cm piece fresh root ginger, peeled and roughly chopped
2 tsp mustard seeds
1 tsp ground turmeric
½ tsp ground coriander

1 green pepper, deseeded and cut into cubes
4 skinless chicken breasts, cut into bite-size pieces
400ml chicken stock
150g fat-free Greek yoghurt
Small bunch of fresh coriander, chopped
Brown rice, to serve

Place the onion, garlic and ginger in a small blender and blend until smooth.

Tip the paste into a frying pan with 2–3 tbsp water and cook for 5 minutes. Stir in the spices and green pepper and cook for a further 2–3 minutes, before adding the chicken and stock. Mix well, then cover and simmer for 10–12 minutes, or until the chicken is cooked through.

Remove from the heat and stir in the yoghurt and half the coriander.

Serve with cooked brown rice and sprinkle with the remaining coriander.

✗ ·

If you're in the Cruise PV phase, you can eat this curry without the rice. If you're in the Stabilization phase, you could add 50g ground almonds with the chicken and stock and garnish the korma with 2 tablespoons toasted flaked almonds just before serving.

· ·

CURRIED CHICKEN
WITH COLESLAW

Serves 4 Preparation time: 20 minutes + marinating Cooking time: 12–16 minutes

consolidation

stabilization

I've found there are lots of ways of making plain old chicken breasts more exciting for the Dukan diet. Even in the Attack phase, you could enjoy these spicy chicken slices without the rice and coleslaw.

2 garlic cloves, peeled and crushed
Juice of 1 lemon
1 tsp paprika
1 tsp medium curry powder
1 tsp ground cumin
Pinch of cayenne pepper
1 tsp ground turmeric
Seasoning
4 skinless chicken breasts

225g white cabbage, shredded
225g carrots, peeled and grated
4 spring onions, finely sliced
2 tbsp fat-free natural yoghurt
2 tbsp extra-light cream cheese
1 tbsp smooth mustard
2 tbsp chopped fresh coriander leaves
Brown rice, to serve

Mix together the garlic, lemon juice, paprika, curry powder, cumin, cayenne, turmeric and seasoning and rub all over the chicken breasts. Place in a non-metallic bowl, cover and leave to marinate in the fridge for at least 1 hour.

To make the coleslaw, place the cabbage, carrots and spring onions in a large bowl. Mix together the yoghurt, cream cheese and mustard, loosening with a little water if needed, then stir into the vegetables.

When ready to cook the chicken, use 3 drops of oil to grease a griddle pan lightly and wipe off with kitchen paper, then heat until really hot. Cook the chicken breasts for 6–8 minutes on each side, until cooked through.

Slice the chicken, if you wish, and serve on a bed of cooked brown rice with the coleslaw on the side.

✗ ···

This very spicy chicken could be eaten in the Cruise phase without the rice.

· ·

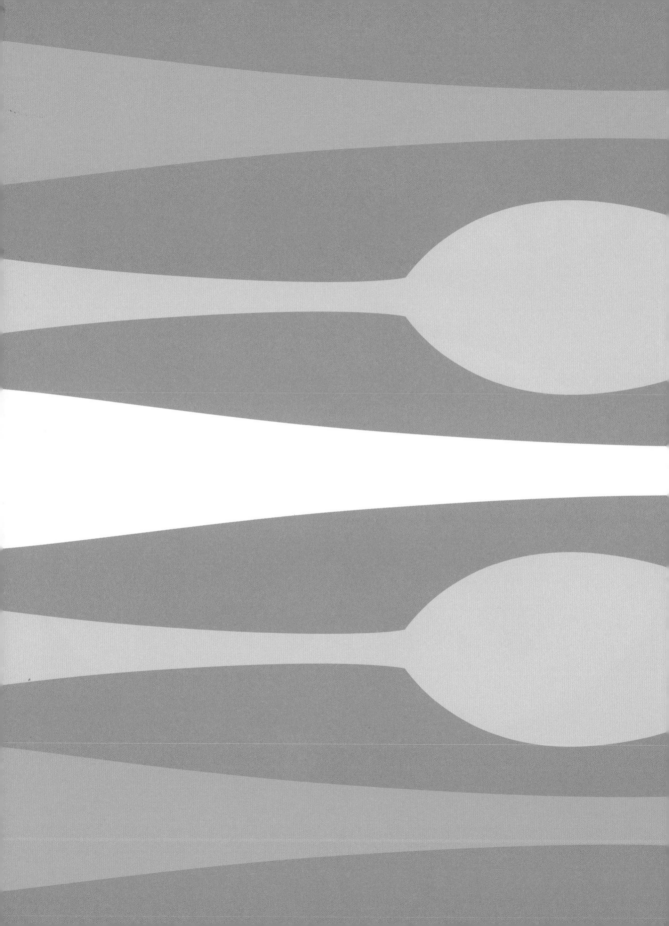

MEATY MEALS

SPICY BEEF-STUFFED PEPPERS

Serves 4 Preparation time: 15 minutes Cooking time: 35 minutes

cruise pv

consolidation

stabilization

Peppers are perfect for being stuffed as they hold their shape really well, but also add a great sweetness to the dish. I think this would be wonderful served at a summer garden lunch, when peppers are at their best.

4 large red or yellow peppers
400g minced beef
1 small onion, peeled and finely chopped
2 garlic cloves, peeled and crushed
1 stick of celery, finely diced
1 courgette, finely diced

1–2 tsp chilli flakes
200g tin chopped tomatoes
1 tsp dried oregano
Seasoning
50g reduced-fat Emmental cheese, grated

Preheat the oven to 200°C/400°F/Gas 6.

Halve the peppers lengthways and remove the seeds. Place on a baking sheet or in a roasting tray and bake in the oven for 15 minutes.

Meanwhile, heat a non-stick frying pan and dry-fry the minced beef with the onion, garlic, celery, courgette and chilli flakes for 4–5 minutes, browning the mince all over. Stir in the chopped tomatoes, oregano and seasoning.

Remove the pepper halves from the oven and spoon the filling into each one. Cover with foil and bake for 12–15 minutes.

Sprinkle with the cheese and bake for a further 5 minutes, until the cheese has melted.

 . . . .

Red and yellow peppers are much sweeter than green, so always use these for this dish if possible.

. . . .

WARM CABBAGE SALAD
WITH SEARED BEEF

Serves 4 Preparation time: **15 minutes** Cooking time: **16-19 minutes**

cruise pv

consolidation

stabilization

I love cabbage, so will find any excuse to add it to a recipe! This salad is also delicious if a little desiccated coconut is added, just to give a bit of extra flavour — but save that idea for when you are in the Stabilization phase.

1 tsp mustard seeds
1 tsp cumin seeds
1 red onion, peeled and finely sliced
2 carrots, peeled and cut into thin
   matchsticks

½ Savoy cabbage, shredded
1 tbsp white wine vinegar
Seasoning
2 x 225g sirloin steaks

Heat 3 drops of oil in a non-stick frying pan or wok and wipe off with kitchen paper. Cook the mustard seeds and cumin seeds until the mustard seeds start to 'pop'.

Add the onion and carrots and cook for a further 2–3 minutes before adding the cabbage and vinegar. Stir-fry for 5–6 minutes until the cabbage is tender, yet still has a bite. Cover and keep warm.

Heat a griddle pan until very hot. Season the steaks, then cook on the hot griddle for 3–4 minutes on each side, depending on how you like your beef. Leave to rest for 4–5 minutes before slicing.

Sprinkling over some pomegranate seeds at the end is delicious if you are in Consolidation.

GRILLED CALF'S LIVER
WITH PUY LENTILS

Serves 4 Preparation time: **15 minutes** Cooking time: **35 minutes**

Liver is an acquired taste, but it is also a very healthy food. This recipe might just convert you! Try not to overcook the liver as this is what makes it tough — it should be very tender.

consolidation

stabilization

110g puy lentils
1 carrot, peeled and diced
1 stick of celery, diced
½ small red onion, peeled and finely diced
4 fresh sage leaves
1 garlic clove, peeled and sliced

Seasoning
100g baby spinach leaves
2–3 tbsp low-fat crème fraîche
4 rashers light bacon
375g calf's liver

Place the lentils, carrot, celery, red onion, sage and garlic in a pan and cover with water. Bring to the boil and simmer for 30 minutes, until the lentils are tender.

Drain the lentils then return to the pan and stir in the seasoning, spinach and crème fraîche. Keep warm.

Meanwhile, grill the bacon until crisp, then roughly chop.

Season the liver and grill or cook on a griddle for 12 minutes on each side — do not overcook as this will make the liver very tough.

Serve the liver on a bed of lentils, sprinkled with crisp bits of bacon.

COTTAGE PIE

Serves 6 Preparation time: 15 minutes Cooking time: 55 minutes

A real family favourite, but this time one you can have whilst losing weight and still sticking to Dukan principles. I think you'll find this butternut squash and cauliflower topping is even tastier than the traditional potato and you can vary the topping too — cooked swede mashed with leeks makes a great alternative that you can also enjoy in the Cruise phase.

cruise pv

consolidation

stabilization

3 rashers light bacon, chopped
1 large onion, peeled and chopped
800g minced beef
2 sprigs of fresh thyme
400g tin chopped tomatoes
2 tsp Worcestershire sauce

350g butternut squash, peeled and chopped
500g cauliflower, chopped
Seasoning
2 tbsp virtually fat-free quark
40g reduced-fat Emmental cheese, grated
Steamed green vegetables, to serve

Preheat the oven to 200°C/400°F/Gas 6.

Dry-fry the bacon for 2–3 minutes before adding the onion and minced beef.

Cook briefly, then add the thyme and pour in the chopped tomatoes, 200ml water and the Worcestershire sauce. Bring to the boil and simmer for 25–30 minutes, stirring occasionally.

Meanwhile, cook the butternut and cauliflower in a pan of boiling water until tender. Drain, season and mash with the quark.

Spoon the beef into an ovenproof dish and top with the mashed butternut and cauliflower. Sprinkle over the grated cheese.

Bake in the oven for 15–20 minutes, then serve with steamed green vegetables.

BEEF & MUSHROOM GOULASH

Serves 4 Preparation time: **10 minutes** Cooking time: **50–55 minutes**

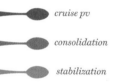

cruise pv

consolidation

stabilization

Goulash is a traditional Hungarian rich meat stew, which is always generously seasoned with paprika. This is a really comforting dish, but without the heaviness I often associate with comfort food, and is perfect for a winter's evening. A great dish for the whole family to eat, served with rice for anyone not following Dukan.

600g sirloin steak, trimmed of fat
   and cut into strips
1 onion, peeled and sliced
1 red pepper, deseeded and sliced
200g chestnut mushrooms, sliced
2 tbsp tomato purée

200ml beef stock
3 tbsp paprika
Seasoning
100g fat-free fromage frais and
   a small bunch of fresh parsley,
   chopped, to serve

Heat 3 drops of oil in a non-stick pan and wipe off with kitchen paper. Heat the pan until very hot and then brown the steak — you may have to do this in batches. Remove with a slotted spoon.

In the same pan, sauté the onion and pepper for 6–8 minutes.

Return the steak to the pan and add the mushrooms, tomato purée, stock, paprika and seasoning and bring to the boil. Simmer for 30–35 minutes, until the meat is very tender.

Serve topped with a dollop of fromage frais and a sprinkling of chopped parsley, along with brown rice if you're in the Consolidation phase.

PORK FILLET
WITH FENNEL & GARLIC

Serves 4 Preparation time: **20 minutes** Cooking time: **1 hour**

consolidation

stabilization

Pork fillet is also known as tenderloin. It's a lazy muscle, which is what makes it so lean and tender. Here it is combined with flavoursome fennel and garlic. Serve with mashed potato for anyone not on Dukan.

3 tbsp fennel seeds
2 garlic cloves, peeled and crushed
1 tbsp fresh thyme leaves
Seasoning
500g pork fillet, trimmed of any fat

2 fennel bulbs, trimmed and sliced
3 red onions, peeled and cut into wedges
2 pears, cored and cut into wedges
300ml vegetable stock
2 tsp cornflour

Preheat the oven to 200°C/400°F/Gas 6.

In a pestle and mortar, grind together the fennel seeds, garlic, thyme and seasoning. Rub the mixture all over the pork fillet.

Heat a non-stick frying pan until hot and brown the pork all over before placing in a roasting tray. Heat 3 drops of oil in the frying pan and wipe off with kitchen paper. Fry the bulb fennel and red onions for 3–4 minutes. Add the fennel and onions to the roasting tray along with the pears and roast in the oven for 35–40 minutes, until the pork is cooked through.

Remove from the oven, take the pork and vegetables out of the roasting tray and keep warm. Place the tray on the hob and pour in the stock. Mix the cornflour with a little water and stir into the stock, scraping away any bits that have been left in the tray from the pork and vegetables. Bring to a simmer and cook for 3–4 minutes until slightly thickened.

Slice the pork and serve on a bed of the roast vegetables and pears, with a spoonful of gravy poured over the top.

STIR-FRY BEEF
WITH CARROT & CHINESE CABBAGE

Serves 4 Preparation time: **10 minutes** Cooking time: **25 minutes**

consolidation

stabilization

Another great beef recipe, this time flavoured with orange — a perfect union. And with the addition of crunchy cabbage and carrot, this is the kind of dish I find pleases the whole family. Be sure to buy only the leanest of beef — ask your butcher for the best cuts. As you are now in the Consolidation or Stabilization phase, you can add brown rice as a side dish or try it with the Egg & Vegetable Fried Rice (page 57).

2 rashers light bacon, cut into strips
1 large onion, peeled and thickly sliced
400g lean steak, cut into strips
2 large carrots, peeled and thinly sliced
½ Chinese cabbage, shredded

1 tbsp orange juice
Grated zest of ½ orange
2 tsp cornflour
1 tsp soy sauce
2 tbsp torn fresh coriander leaves

Dry-fry the bacon in a wok for 1 minute before adding the onion and steak. Continue to stir-fry for 6–7 minutes.

Add the carrots and cabbage and stir-fry for 2–3 minutes.

Mix the orange juice and zest with 200ml water and pour into the wok. Bring to the boil, then simmer for 8–10 minutes, stirring occasionally.

Mix the cornflour with the soy sauce and a little water, then pour into the wok and stir until the sauce starts to thicken.

Stir in the chopped coriander and serve.

✕ ·

If you omit the orange juice, this dish can be eaten in the Cruise PV phase.

· ·

ITALIAN MEATBALLS
WITH VEGETABLE PASTA

Serves 4 Preparation time: **25 minutes** Cooking time: **40 minutes**

cruise

consolidation

stabilization

These strips of carrot and courgette are a delicious and clever way of eating healthy vegetables with your meatballs. And steaming them is a gentle method of cooking that helps to retain the nutrients.

For the meatballs
250g minced beef
250g minced pork fillet
1 egg
1 garlic clove, peeled and crushed
1 tsp dried oregano
2–3 tbsp oat bran
Seasoning

For the tomato sauce
1 onion, peeled and chopped

1 garlic clove, peeled
1 tsp dried oregano
½ tbsp olive oil
400g tin chopped tomatoes
100ml skimmed milk

For the vegetable pasta
2 carrots
3 courgettes
2 tbsp grated Parmesan cheese

To make the meatballs, place all the ingredients in a large bowl and, using your hands, mix together really well before shaping into small walnut-sized balls. Place the meatballs on a plate and chill while you make the tomato sauce.

To make the tomato sauce, place the onion, garlic and oregano in a small blender and blend until smooth.

Heat the olive oil in a pan and cook the onion mixture for 8–10 minutes, stirring occasionally. Add the chopped tomatoes with 100ml water, bring to the boil and then simmer for 10 minutes — the sauce will gradually thicken.

Meanwhile, heat 3 drops of oil in a non-stick frying pan and wipe off with kitchen paper. Cook the meatballs, turning frequently, for 5–6 minutes.

Stir the milk into the tomato sauce, bring to a simmer and add the meatballs. Continue to cook for 8–10 minutes.

For the pasta, use a vegetable peeler or mandolin to cut the carrots and courgettes into thin strips, then halve them lengthways to look like thick tagliatelle. Steam the strips for 4–6 minutes until tender. If you don't have a steamer, place them in a colander over a pan of simmering water and cover with a lid to trap in the steam. Divide the vegetable pasta among four warmed shallow bowls.

Spoon the meatballs and tomato sauce over the vegetable pasta and serve (if you are past the Attack and Cruise phases) sprinkled with a little grated Parmesan.

If you have reached Stabilization, you can have these tasty meatballs with real wheat spaghetti and Parmesan. Or you could try konjac shiritaki noodles – especially in the Cruise phase. You can buy them in health food shops and at mydukandietshop.co.uk.

SPAGHETTI BOLOGNESE

Serves 4 Preparation time: 10 minutes Cooking time: 25 minutes

consolidation

stabilization

A real family favourite that had to be included. This recipe shows you that everyday foods you thought you would have to go without are still possible on the Dukan Diet.

½ tbsp vegetable oil
4 rashers light bacon, roughly chopped
500g minced beef
1 onion, peeled and chopped
1 carrot, peeled and diced
2 sticks of celery, diced
2 garlic cloves, peeled and crushed

400g tin chopped tomatoes
½ tsp dried oregano
Seasoning
400g wholewheat spaghetti
2 tbsp grated Parmesan cheese
1 tbsp chopped fresh parsley

Heat the oil in a frying pan and fry the bacon for 3–4 minutes. Add the minced beef and cook for 3–4 minutes over a high heat to brown.

Add the onion, carrot, celery and garlic and cook over a medium heat for 1–2 minutes before adding the chopped tomatoes, oregano, seasoning and 100ml water. Bring to the boil and then simmer for 12–15 minutes, stirring occasionally, until thick.

Meanwhile, bring a large pan of water to the boil and cook the spaghetti for 10 minutes, or according to the pack instructions, until *al dente* (tender, but with a bit of a bite). Drain the pasta and divide among four warmed shallow dishes or plates.

Spoon the Bolognese sauce over the pasta and serve immediately, sprinkled with grated Parmesan cheese and chopped parsley.

If you are still in the Cruise phase, serve the Bolognese sauce with some steamed vegetables of your choice or konjac shiritaki noodles rather than the pasta, or you could make the vegetable pasta described in Italian Meatballs with Vegetable Pasta (page 113).

ROSEMARY & GARLIC ROASTED LEG OF LAMB
WITH BUTTER BEANS

Serves 6-8 Preparation time: **10 minutes** Cooking time: **1½ hours**

Perfect for a large family gathering, this leg of lamb will serve around six guests and is also delicious cold if you happen to have any left over! If you need a Sunday roast or Easter Sunday recipe when you're on Stabilization or Consolidation, this is the one I'd reach for.

consolidation

stabilization

2.5kg leg of lamb
4 sprigs of fresh rosemary, broken
   into small sprigs
4 garlic cloves, peeled and sliced
4 red onions, peeled and cut into wedges

2 x 400g tins butter beans,
   drained and rinsed
16 cherry tomatoes
Steamed green vegetables, to serve

Preheat the oven to 220°C/425°F/Gas 7. Make deep incisions all over the leg of lamb using a small knife. Push small sprigs of rosemary and slices of garlic into the cuts. Place in a roasting tray with the wedges of red onion and roast in the oven for 15 minutes before reducing the oven temperature to 180°C/350°F/Gas 4. Cook for another hour.

Add the butter beans and tomatoes to the tray and roast for a further 15 minutes.

To test if the lamb is cooked, pierce at the thickest part with a sharp knife — if the juices run clear, the meat is cooked.

Leave the lamb to rest for about 10-15 minutes before carving and serving. Serve with steamed green vegetables.

When serving roasted meat, always leave to rest before carving — the meat still continues to cook when first taken out of the oven and resting enables it to hold on to more moisture.

CHUMP OF LAMB
WITH GREMOLATA

Serves 4 Preparation time: 20 minutes + marinating Cooking time: 15 minutes

consolidation

stabilization

Lamb chump is the cut just next to the leg and can be eaten from the Consolidation phase onwards. It is a tasty, cheap cut of lamb and very easy to cook.

Grated zest of 2 large lemons
Large bunch of fresh rosemary,
   finely chopped
Large bunch of fresh parsley,
   finely chopped
4 garlic cloves, peeled and crushed

1 tsp olive oil
Seasoning
4 lamb chump chops
16 cherry tomatoes, halved
200g green beans, trimmed

To make the gremolata, mix together the lemon zest, rosemary, parsley, garlic, olive oil and seasoning and stir together well.

Place half of the gremolata into a large plastic food bag with the chump chops and mix thoroughly. Leave to marinate for at least 2 hours or overnight if you wish.

Preheat the oven to 200°C/400°F/Gas 6.

Heat a non-stick frying pan and sear the chump chops for 2–3 minutes on each side, then place in a roasting tray with the tomatoes and sprinkle the remaining gremolata over the lamb. Roast in the oven for 7–8 minutes.

Meanwhile, steam the green beans.

Serve the lamb and tomatoes on a bed of green beans.

FISH FAVOURITES

SALMON & SQUASH FISH CAKES

Serves 4 Preparation time: **20 minutes** + chilling Cooking time: **25 minutes**

consolidation

stabilization

Traditional fish cakes contain potato to bind them, but this recipe uses butternut squash or pumpkin so they are a little softer, but just as tasty. I find fish cakes are great for using up leftover fish — try this recipe with cod or haddock too.

500g butternut squash,
   peeled and chopped
315g salmon fillet
3 tbsp oat bran
Seasoning
1 tbsp chopped fresh dill

2 slices wholemeal bread,
   made into crumbs
1 tbsp sesame seeds
2 tbsp wholemeal flour
1 egg, beaten
Steamed green vegetables or green salad,
   to serve

Steam the butternut for 8–10 minutes, or until tender. If you don't have a steamer, place it in a colander over a pan of simmering water and cover with a lid to trap in the steam. Transfer to a bowl and roughly mash with a fork.

Steam the salmon for 6 minutes, then flake with a fork and add to the butternut. Leave to cool for 5 minutes. Sprinkle in the oat bran, seasoning and dill and mix well. Using wet hands, form the mixture into four fish cakes.

Mix the breadcrumbs with the sesame seeds and place in a shallow bowl. Place the flour and egg in two separate bowls. Dip each fishcake first into the flour, then in the egg and finally in the breadcrumbs and sesame seeds to coat. Chill for 10–15 minutes.

Heat 3 drops of oil in a non-stick frying pan and wipe off with kitchen paper. Cook the fish cakes for 5–6 minutes on each side, until crisp and golden.

Serve with steamed green vegetables or a green salad.

✗ ·

Once you are in the Stabilization phase, you can swap half the butternut with potato if you wish.

· ·

MACKEREL & POTATO SALAD

Serves 4 Preparation time: **12 minutes** Cooking time: **25 minutes**

Mackerel is a really healthy fish to include in your diet as it is rich in omega fats that are needed for healthy cells and brain function. It's my favourite fish and is cheap to buy, so I eat it on a regular basis. Ask your local fishmonger to fillet it for you too.

350g new potatoes, halved if large
400g Savoy cabbage, shredded
2 tsp horseradish sauce
100ml low-fat crème fraîche
4 mackerel fillets
Juice of ½ lemon
Black pepper
4 wedges of lemon, to serve

Cook the potatoes in a pan of boiling water for 12–15 minutes, until tender.

Steam the cabbage for 4–5 minutes. If you don't have a steamer, place the cabbage in a colander over a pan of simmering water and cover with a lid to trap in the steam.

Drain the potatoes, return to the warm pan and lightly crush with a fork. Stir in the cabbage, horseradish and crème fraîche and keep warm whilst you cook the mackerel.

Place the mackerel fillets in a griddle pan, squeeze over the lemon juice and season with black pepper. Griddle for 3–4 minutes on each side until cooked through.

Divide the warm potato salad among four warmed plates and top with a mackerel fillet and a wedge of lemon.

✕ ·

To enjoy mackerel in the Cruise phase, try it grilled and served on a bed of steamed spinach.

· ·

stabilization

ORIENTAL CRAB OMELETTE

Serves 1 Preparation time: 15 minutes Cooking time: 2-3 minutes

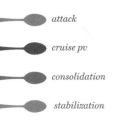

attack

cruise pv

consolidation

stabilization

This delicious crab omelette has been jazzed up with the addition of a few oriental spices. If you prefer your food to be less spicy, omit the green chilli, which gives the heat to the dish. If you cannot find fresh crab, frozen crabmeat is just as tasty.

½ green chilli, deseeded and diced
150g white crabmeat
2 tsp grated fresh root ginger
3 spring onions, finely sliced
3 eggs
2 tsp soy sauce

Mix together the chilli, crabmeat, ginger and half the spring onions.

Lightly beat the eggs with the soy sauce.

Heat 3 drops of oil in a non-stick frying pan over a medium heat and wipe off with kitchen paper. Pour in the egg mixture and gently stir with a fork to allow all of the egg to cook.

After around 2 minutes, the omelette should be cooked enough to turn out onto a plate. Sprinkle the crab mixture down the middle of the omelette and roll up.

Slice in half and serve sprinkled with the remaining spring onions.

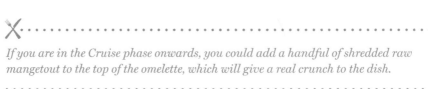

If you are in the Cruise phase onwards, you could add a handful of shredded raw mangetout to the top of the omelette, which will give a real crunch to the dish.

SALADE NIÇOISE

Serves 4 Preparation time: 20 minutes Cooking time: 20 minutes

The harissa paste in the dressing adds a little bit of spicy heat, and an interesting twist to this classic salad, but you can omit it if you wish. Even when you have removed the tuna from the pan, it will still continue to cook from its residual heat, so be careful not to overcook as this makes tuna very tough.

cruise pv

consolidation

stabilization

450g tuna steaks
125g butternut squash, peeled and
  cut into bite-size chunks
125g green beans, trimmed
4 little gem lettuces
4 hard-boiled eggs, peeled and
  cut into quarters
4 tomatoes, roughly chopped
1 red onion, peeled and finely sliced

6 tinned anchovy fillets, chopped
4–5 fresh basil leaves, roughly torn
1 egg yolk
4 tbsp balsamic vinegar
3 tbsp fat-free fromage frais
1 tbsp chopped fresh chives
½ tsp harissa paste
Seasoning

Heat 3 drops of oil in a griddle pan and wipe off with kitchen paper. Cook the tuna steaks for 2–3 minutes on each side, depending on how rare you like your fish. Remove from the pan and set aside.

Cook the butternut squash in a pan of boiling water for 12–15 minutes until tender, adding the green beans 2 minutes before the end of the cooking time. Drain and refresh under cold water.

Break the leaves of the lettuces apart and place on a large platter. Scatter over the squash, beans, hard-boiled eggs, tomatoes, red onion, anchovy fillets and torn basil leaves. Break up the tuna into big flakes and scatter over the salad.

Whisk together the egg yolk, balsamic vinegar, fromage frais, chives, harissa and seasoning and pour this dressing over the salad to serve.

If you are in the Stabilization phase, 10 small new potatoes can be included instead of the squash.

RED MULLET & LEEKS EN PAPILLOTE

Makes 4 Preparation time: **15 minutes** Cooking time: **15-20 minutes**

I find baking fish in greaseproof paper is a great way of cooking without the need for oil and, as it is gentle, it helps to retain nutrients and flavour. Even better, you can prepare the dish in advance, then just pop it in the oven when you are ready.

cruise pv

consolidation

stabilization

300g baby spinach leaves
2 medium leeks, washed, trimmed and very thinly sliced
4 tbsp low-fat crème fraîche
8 red mullet fillets
1 lime, sliced
Seasoning

Preheat the oven to 200°C/400°F/Gas 6.

Cut eight pieces of greaseproof paper into squares large enough to cover each fillet plus a 3–4cm border. Lightly brush four of the squares of paper with 3 drops of oil. In the centre of each square of paper, lay a quarter of the spinach, a quarter of the leeks, 1 tablespoon crème fraîche, 2 red mullet fillets, a couple of slices of lime and some seasoning.

Lay the other greaseproof squares on top of the fillets and fold up the edges to form pockets. Place the pockets on a baking sheet and bake in the oven for 15–20 minutes.

Serve hot, allowing the diners to open the paper pockets at the table and enjoy the lovely aroma as they do so.

 . . . .

If you are still in the Attack phase, you can cook your fish this way just by adding a little seasoning, herbs and lemon juice.

. . . .

KEDGEREE

Serves 4 Preparation time: **15 minutes** Cooking time: **1 hour**

consolidation

stabilization

Aficionados of the quintessential kedgeree insist that it should be made with smoked haddock, but I find it also works well with other smoked or unsmoked fish and could even include seafood if you prefer — make to your own taste.

350g smoked haddock
1 large onion, peeled and chopped
2 tsp curry powder
½ tsp ground turmeric
175g brown rice, rinsed
1 tbsp tomato purée

225g baby spinach leaves
4 tbsp fat-free Greek yoghurt
Seasoning
4 hard-boiled eggs, peeled and
    cut into quarters
2 tbsp chopped fresh parsley

Bring 1.2 litres water to the boil, add the smoked haddock and simmer for 3–4 minutes. Remove the fish with a slotted spoon, reserving the cooking liquid.

Heat 3 drops of oil in a large non-stick frying pan or wok and wipe off with kitchen paper. Sauté the onion for 2–3 minutes before stirring in the spices and cooking for another 2 minutes.

Stir in the rice and tomato purée and mix well. Add the reserved cooking liquid and bring to the boil. Cover and simmer for 40–45 minutes, until the rice is tender and all liquid has evaporated. Stir in the spinach until it is wilted.

Flake the fish and gently stir into the rice with the yoghurt, seasoning, eggs and parsley, then serve immediately.

HADDOCK FLORENTINE

Serves 4 Preparation time: **10 minutes** Cooking time: **10 minutes**

cruise pv

consolidation

stabilization

This version of eggs Florentine uses haddock, but it's also great with salmon, cod or any other chunky fish fillet you prefer. The Florentine can be served on English muffins for those not on the diet or on slices of wholemeal bread for those in the Consolidation phase.

1kg fresh spinach
50g extra-light cream cheese
100g fat-free fromage frais
1–2 tbsp skimmed milk

Grated zest of 1 lemon
Seasoning
4 eggs
4 haddock fillets, skinned

Wash the spinach, then place in a large pan with just the residual water to cook over a medium heat until wilted. Drain and keep warm.

Whisk together the cream cheese, fromage frais, milk, lemon zest and seasoning and heat for 1 minute in a microwave.

Meanwhile, bring a frying pan of water to a simmer and gently drop in the 4 eggs. Poach for 5–6 minutes (depending on how well done you like your eggs), then remove with a slotted spoon and keep warm.

Grill the fish for 3–4 minutes on each side, until cooked through.

Divide the spinach among four warmed plates or shallow bowls and top with the grilled fish, and then a poached egg. Spoon over the cheesy lemon sauce to serve.

Don't add extra water when cooking spinach – just the residual water from washing will be enough, otherwise you will have too much liquid in the finished dish.

FISH & CHIPS

Serves 1 Preparation time: 15 minutes Cooking time: 15 minutes

cruise pv

consolidation

stabilization

I had to include this recipe as Fish and Chips is certainly a favourite of mine, even when I am trying to be healthy. You may be on a diet, but there is no reason why you can't have a Friday night treat!

2 tbsp oat bran
1 tbsp chopped fresh tarragon
1 tsp chopped fresh parsley
Seasoning
1 cod loin
2 tbsp cornflour

1 egg, beaten
125g butternut squash, peeled
   and cut into chips
1 large carrot, peeled and cut into chips
½ tbsp capers, drained
2 tbsp fat-free natural yoghurt

Preheat the oven to 200°C/400°F/Gas 6.

Mix together the oat bran with the chopped tarragon and parsley. Season well.

Dip the cod loin first into the cornflour, then the egg and finally the herby oat bran. Place on a baking sheet and bake in the oven for 12–14 minutes, until the fish is cooked through.

Meanwhile, steam the butternut and carrot chips for 8–10 minutes until tender. If you don't have a steamer, place them in a colander over a pan of simmering water and cover with a lid to trap in the steam.

Chop the capers and stir into the yoghurt.

Serve the fish and chips with the capered yoghurt on the side.

GRILLED DOVER SOLE
WITH SALSA VERDE

Serves 4 Preparation time: **15 minutes** Cooking time: **10 minutes**

Salsa verde is a classic Italian sauce, which literally translates to 'green sauce'. It is a great sauce to have up one's sleeve on the diet and here I serve it with grilled Dover sole, but it is also good with other fish or even a grilled steak. This is delicious with new potatoes if you're cooking for people not following Dukan.

cruise pv

consolidation

stabilization

1 garlic clove, peeled
4 tinned anchovy fillets
1 shallot, peeled and chopped
Grated zest and juice of 1 lemon
2 tbsp capers, drained and
  roughly chopped

Small bunch of fresh parsley
Small bunch of fresh basil
Seasoning
4 Dover sole

Using a pestle and mortar, crush the garlic with the anchovies until you have a rough paste, then add the shallot and lemon zest and crush a little more.

Stir in the capers, herbs and half the lemon juice and crush just a little to bring out the flavour of the herbs.

Season well and add a little water to loosen if wished.

Wash the Dover sole and pat dry with kitchen paper. Season the fish on each side with the remaining lemon juice and some black pepper.

Preheat the grill. Wipe the grill pan with 3 drops of oil and wipe off with kitchen paper. Grill the sole for 4–5 minutes on each side, according to the thickness of the fish, then serve on warmed plates with a drizzle of the salsa verde.

If you are still in the Attack phase, serve the fish just lightly seasoned and grilled.

SEAFOOD PASTA

Serves 4 Preparation time: 15 minutes Cooking time: 10 minutes

This is a wonderful summer dish, when seafood is abundant in this country, and is one of those perfect summer holiday recipes to make if you're staying by the sea. Vary the seafood you use, depending on what is available.

consolidation

stabilization

250g wholewheat spaghetti
2 spring onions, sliced
4 garlic cloves, peeled and sliced
1 tsp chilli flakes
Grated zest and juice of 1 lemon

24 cooked king prawns, peeled
12 cooked mussels (without shells)
2 tbsp chopped fresh parsley
Seasoning
Rocket leaves, to serve

Cook the spaghetti in a pan of boiling water for 8–10 minutes, until *al dente* (tender, but with a bite).

Meanwhile, heat 3 drops of oil in a non-stick frying pan and wipe off with kitchen paper. Cook the spring onions, garlic, chilli and lemon zest for 2 minutes.

Add the prawns and mussels to the frying pan and cook for 2 minutes.

Drain the pasta and toss into the seafood pan along with the lemon juice, parsley and seasoning.

Serve with rocket.

Saffron goes really well with seafood — just add a little pinch instead of the chilli for a completely different dish.

FISH PIE

Serves 4 Preparation time: **30 minutes** Cooking time: **35 minutes**

cruise pv

consolidation

stabilization

A real family meal, fish pie can include so many different flavours: prawns, eggs, smoked fish, different herbs and different toppings — the variations are endless. Use this recipe as your basic guide, then change the ingredients to suit yourself and your family.

400g cod fillets
400g salmon fillets
500ml skimmed milk
2 shallots, peeled and halved
4 cloves
2 bay leaves
4 eggs
100g cooked prawns

400g fat-free natural yoghurt
Seasoning
Small bunch of fresh parsley, chopped
250g baby spinach leaves
3 leeks, washed, trimmed and sliced
75g reduced-fat Emmental cheese, grated
Steamed green vegetables,
  to serve (optional)

Preheat the oven to 200°C/400°F/Gas 6.

Place the fish in a frying pan and pour over the milk. Stud each shallot half with a clove and add these to the pan along with the bay leaves. Bring to the boil and simmer for 6–8 minutes, until the fish is cooked through. Remove the fish with a slotted spoon, flake into large chunks and place them into an ovenproof dish. Reserve the milk.

Hard-boil the eggs in a small pan of water, then immediately run under cold water to cease the cooking process. Peel the eggs, cut into quarters and arrange in the ovenproof dish with the fish. Sprinkle over the cooked prawns.

Whisk together the natural yoghurt and 250ml of the milk used for cooking the fish. Season and stir in the chopped parsley, then pour over the fish.

Wash the baby spinach leaves and place in a pan with just the residual water, cover and cook for 3–4 minutes until wilted. Squeeze out the excess moisture, then sprinkle the spinach over the fish.

Steam the leeks for 4–5 minutes until tender and sprinkle them over the spinach. If you don't have a steamer, place the leeks in a colander over a pan of simmering water and cover with a lid to trap in the steam.

Finish off the dish by sprinkling over the grated cheese. Bake in the oven for 15 minutes to make sure everything is heated through and the cheese is bubbling and golden.

Serve with steamed green vegetables, if wished.

If you are in the Attack phase, serve yourself the fish and sauce separately before adding the topping for the other diners.

ROAST COD & RATATOUILLE

Serves 4 Preparation time: 15 minutes Cooking time: 50 minutes

cruise pv

consolidation

stabilization

This dish can all be made in one roasting tray and is a very simple but nutritious meal the whole family can enjoy together. Other fish could also be used — salmon, haddock or pollack all work really well cooked this way.

1 small aubergine, cut into cubes
2 courgettes, sliced
450g ripe plum tomatoes, roughly
 chopped
1 red pepper, deseeded and chopped
1 yellow pepper, deseeded and chopped

1 red onion, peeled and cut into wedges
3 garlic cloves, peeled and sliced
Handful of fresh basil leaves
1 tsp olive oil
Seasoning
4 x 150g cod loins

Preheat the oven to 200°C/400°F/Gas 6.

Place all the vegetables in a large shallow roasting tray and sprinkle with the garlic, roughly torn basil leaves, olive oil and seasoning.

Roast in the oven on the highest shelf for 35–40 minutes, tossing the vegetables halfway through the cooking time.

Place the cod loins on top of the vegetables and cook for a further 10–12 minutes, until the fish is cooked through.

Serve the cod on a bed of roasted ratatouille.

If you are in the Consolidation or Stabilization phases, you could add 50g grated Manchego cheese to the cod just before you cook the fish.

CRAB BURGERS

Serves 4 Preparation time: **15 minutes + chilling** Cooking time: **6-8 minutes**

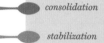

consolidation

stabilization

If you love burgers, but are not keen on having meat too often, I think these delicious crab burgers make a fine substitute. Use both dark and white crabmeat for a great flavour. To toast the sesame seeds, just cook in a dry frying pan and toss around until they start to turn golden.

4 spring onions, finely diced	¼ Chinese cabbage, shredded
450g crabmeat	25g mangetout, shredded
Grated zest and juice of 1 lemon	12 cherry tomatoes, halved
2 tbsp chopped fresh parsley	2 red peppers, deseeded and thinly sliced
2 eggs, beaten	1 tsp olive oil
100g breadcrumbs	2 tbsp sesame seeds, toasted
Seasoning	

In a large bowl, mix together the spring onions, crabmeat, lemon zest, parsley, eggs, breadcrumbs and seasoning.

Using wet hands, shape the mixture into four burgers, then place in the fridge to chill for 20–30 minutes.

Heat 3 drops of oil in a non-stick pan and wipe off with kitchen paper. Cook the burgers for 3–4 minutes on each side, until golden brown.

Meanwhile, toss together the cabbage, mangetout, tomatoes and red peppers with the olive oil and lemon juice.

Serve the burgers on top of the shredded salad, sprinkled with toasted sesame seeds.

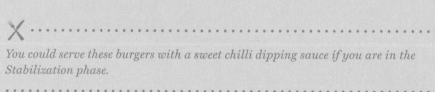

You could serve these burgers with a sweet chilli dipping sauce if you are in the Stabilization phase.

ROAST SALMON
WITH CHICKPEA & RED PEPPER SALAD

Serves 4 Preparation time: **20 minutes** Cooking time: **40-45 minutes**

This is a great mid-week standby and you can enjoy the salmon without the salad if you are in the early stages of the diet. Salmon is a healthy oily fish that can provide a useful intake of omega fats, which are essential for health — not only for great skin and a healthy heart, but also for a well-functioning brain!

consolidation

stabilization

3 red peppers, halved and deseeded
400g tin chickpeas, drained and rinsed
2 tbsp chopped fresh parsley
1 tbsp chopped fresh mint
1 tbsp capers, drained

½ cucumber, chopped
1 garlic clove, peeled and crushed
2 lemons
800g salmon fillet, halved and skin on
½ tsp chilli flakes

Preheat the oven to 200°C/400°F/Gas 6.

Place the peppers on a baking sheet, cut side down, and cook under a hot grill for 12-15 minutes, until they are black.

Place the charred peppers into a bowl, cover with cling film and leave to cool. When they are cool enough to handle, remove the blackened skin and cut the peppers into strips.

Mix the peppers with the chickpeas, herbs, capers, cucumber, garlic and the juice of 1 lemon and leave to stand at room temperature.

Place half the salmon on a piece of baking pepper in a roasting tray, skin side down. Sprinkle over the chilli flakes and then cover with thin slices of the remaining lemon. Place the rest of the salmon on top, skin side up, and fold the paper into a parcel.

Cook in the oven for 25-30 minutes, until the fish is cooked through.

Serve the roast salmon on a bed of chickpea and red pepper salad.

TUNA & LENTIL BAKE

Serves 4 Preparation time: 15 minutes Cooking time: 35 minutes

consolidation

stabilization

A great midweek supper for the whole family. I always have tins of tuna and dried lentils in the cupboard, so this is an easy recipe to put together when I don't want to go shopping!

1 onion, peeled and diced
1 carrot, peeled and diced
1 stick of celery, diced
250g dried red lentils
500ml vegetable stock

130g tin tuna, drained and flaked
2 tbsp chopped fresh chives
1 tbsp chopped fresh parsley
Seasoning
35g reduced-fat Cheddar cheese, grated

Preheat the oven to 200°C/400°F/Gas 6.

Heat 3 drops of oil in a non-stick saucepan and wipe off with kitchen paper. Sauté the onion, carrot and celery for 4–5 minutes until they start to soften.

Stir in the red lentils, then pour in the vegetable stock, bring to the boil and simmer for 12–14 minutes, until the lentils have swollen and soaked up the liquid.

Take off the heat and stir in the tuna, herbs and seasoning. Pour into an ovenproof dish, sprinkle with the cheese and bake in the oven for 15 minutes until the cheese is melted and bubbling. Serve hot.

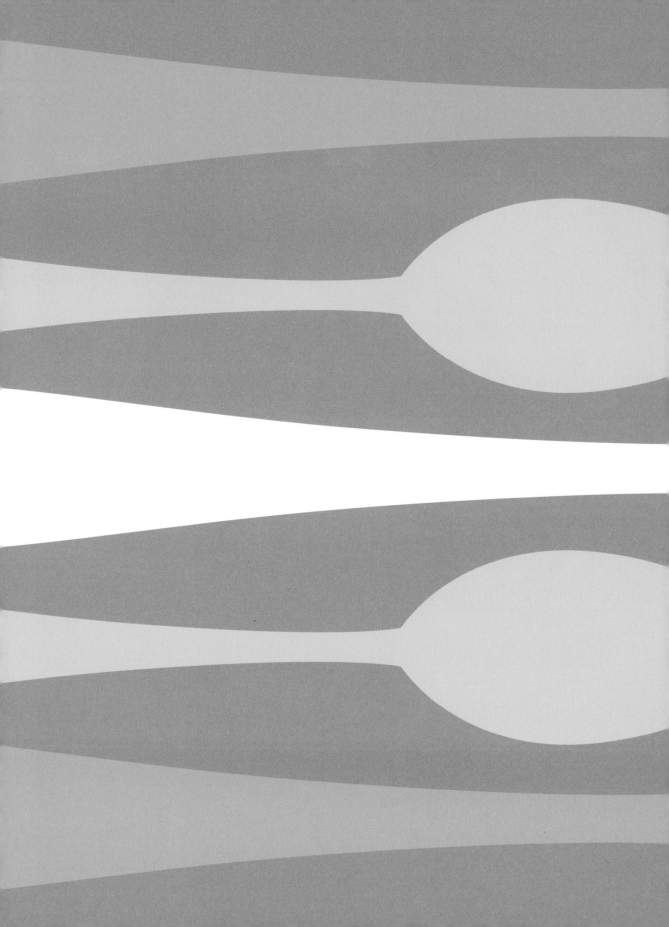

MEAT-FREE FEASTS

ROAST BEETROOT & SPINACH SALAD

Serves 4 Preparation time: **20 minutes** Cooking time: **35 minutes**

If you love beetroot as much as I do, you will love this light, pretty salad. Roasting beetroot is so easy and gives a much deeper flavour than boiling or pickling it. Beetroot is at its best in the late summer, so enjoy this recipe when it is abundant.

cruise pv

consolidation

stabilization

6 medium beetroot, cut into wedges
2 red onions, peeled and cut into
   thick wedges
1 tsp cumin seeds
1 tsp olive oil
Seasoning

150g broccoli florets
½ tbsp balsamic vinegar
2 tsp fresh thyme leaves
200g baby spinach leaves
50g mangetout, shredded

Preheat the oven to 200°C/400°F/Gas 6.

Place the beetroot, red onions, cumin seeds and olive oil in a roasting tray and shake around to coat the vegetables with the oil. Season well and roast in the oven for 30–35 minutes, until the beetroot is tender.

Meanwhile, cook the broccoli in boiling water for 4–5 minutes until tender and then refresh under running cold water. Drain.

Remove the beetroot and onions from the oven. Stir in the balsamic vinegar and thyme and leave to cool slightly.

Toss together the broccoli, spinach and mangetout, then toss together with the beetroot to serve.

✕ . . . .

If you are in the Consolidation or Stabilization phases, you could sprinkle over 350g Manchego cheese cubes.

. . . .

SPICED KALE
WITH FLAGEOLET BEANS

Serves 4 Preparation time: **10 minutes** Cooking time: **20 minutes**

 consolidation

stabilization

Kale is one of those vegetables that look really fresh and healthy, but it can be hard to think of what to do with it. My recipe should fix that!

1 onion, peeled and chopped
2 garlic cloves, peeled and chopped
3 tsp cumin seeds
2 tsp coriander seeds
Pinch of saffron threads
2 tsp paprika
1 red chilli, deseeded and finely chopped
400g kale, shredded

Juice of 1 lemon
100ml vegetable stock
2 x 400g tins flageolet beans,
    drained and rinsed
Seasoning
2 tbsp chopped fresh mint
3 tbsp chopped fresh coriander

Heat 3 drops of oil in a non-stick frying pan and wipe off with kitchen paper. Sauté the onion and garlic for 2–3 minutes before stirring in the spices and chilli and cooking for a further 4–5 minutes, stirring from time to time to prevent sticking.

Add the kale, lemon juice, stock, beans and seasoning. Bring to a simmer and then cook, covered, for 8–10 minutes.

Remove from the heat, stir in the chopped herbs and serve immediately.

RAINBOW FRITTATA

Serves 4-6 Preparation time: **15 minutes** Cooking time: **30 minutes**

Frittatas are great for eating hot or cold and are perfect for taking on a picnic or in a lunch box cut into wedges. This dish is especially useful because you can easily vary the ingredients, using summer vegetables or herbs of your choice.

1 red onion, peeled and thickly sliced
1 red pepper, deseeded and chopped
1 yellow pepper, deseeded and chopped
7 eggs

1 small fennel bulb, trimmed, halved
  and sliced
2 tbsp chopped fresh chives
Seasoning

cruise pv

consolidation

stabilization

Heat 3 drops of oil in a non-stick frying pan and wipe off with kitchen paper. Sauté the onion and peppers for 5–6 minutes.

Lightly beat the eggs in a large bowl, then stir in the cooked onion and peppers and add the remaining ingredients.

Pour the egg and vegetable mixture back into the frying pan and cook over a medium heat for 15–18 minutes, until golden underneath.

Place the frying pan under a hot grill and cook the top of the frittata for a further 5–6 minutes, until the top is golden and cooked.

Place a chopping board or plate over the frying pan and quickly invert it to turn out the frittata. Cut into wedges to serve.

✕ ·

Include peas if you are in the Consolidation phase or use only onion and herbs if you are still in the Attack phase.

· ·

CHARGRILLED COURGETTE & CANNELLINI BEAN SALAD

Serves 4 Preparation time: **15 minutes** Cooking time: **25 minutes**

This is the perfect summer salad as you can even cook the courgettes on the barbecue, without having to make a mess in the kitchen! Chargrilled vegetables are a great idea for the early Cruise phase of the Dukan diet and can be used as an accompaniment or in a warm salad.

consolidation

stabilization

4 courgettes, cut into long thin strips
1 tsp olive oil
1 red chilli, deseeded and finely chopped
Seasoning
Juice of ½ lemon
Handful of fresh mint

Handful of fresh basil
400g tin cannellini beans, drained and rinsed
12 cherry tomatoes, halved
30g watercress
30g rocket

In a large bowl, toss the courgette strips with the olive oil, chilli and seasoning.

Heat a griddle pan until very hot (or you can use the barbecue) and cook the courgette strips in batches, about 3–4 minutes on each side, until they have charred ridge marks. They should be tender but still retain a little crunch.

Toss the courgettes in the bowl with the lemon juice, herbs, beans and tomatoes and serve on a bed of watercress and rocket.

✗ . . . .

Leave out the beans for a Cruise PV recipe.

. . . .

VEGETABLE STIR-FRY
WITH MARINATED TOFU

Serves 4 Preparation time: 25 minutes + marinating Cooking time: 40-45 minutes

*For those people who think tofu has no flavour, think again, as this recipe gives a
real kick to the ingredient. And if you want to add more, you can throw a diced red
chilli into the marinade too. Tofu is a great source of protein, perfect for this diet.
Easy to serve with rice if you're eating with others not on the Dukan.*

cruise pv

consolidation

stabilization

400g tofu, drained and cut into
   bite-size chunks
3–4 tbsp soy sauce
2 garlic cloves, peeled and crushed
1 tbsp grated fresh root ginger
1 tsp sesame oil

1 tbsp rice vinegar
2 red onions, peeled and sliced
2 red peppers, deseeded and sliced
300g chestnut mushrooms, thickly sliced
4 heads of pak choi, cut into quarters
2 tbsp sesame seeds

Place the tofu in a non-metallic container.

Mix together the soy sauce, garlic, ginger, sesame oil and rice vinegar and pour over
the tofu. Cover and leave to marinate for 2–3 hours, or preferably overnight.

Preheat the oven to 180°C/350°F/Gas 4. Use 3 drops of oil to grease a baking sheet
lightly and wipe off with kitchen paper.

Reserving the marinade, place the drained tofu onto the baking sheet and bake
in the oven for 40–45 minutes, turning at least once.

Heat 3 drops of oil in a large non-stick frying pan or wok and wipe off with kitchen
paper. Cook the onions for 2–3 minutes before adding the red peppers and
mushrooms and cooking for a further 3–4 minutes, stirring frequently.

Add the pak choi and reserved marinade, mix well and cook for a further 3–4 minutes.

Serve the vegetables stirred together with the baked tofu and a sprinkling of
sesame seeds.

BUBBLE & SQUEAK
TOPPED WITH POACHED EGG

Serves 4 Preparation time: **20 minutes** Cooking time: **25 minutes**

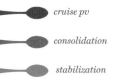

cruise pv

consolidation

stabilization

Another family favourite, usually made with leftover vegetables, but just as easy to make from scratch. This version uses deliciously sweet butternut squash instead of the more usual potato.

500g butternut squash or pumpkin,
  peeled and cut into bite-size chunks
4 spring onions, finely chopped
½ tbsp low-fat crème fraîche

Seasoning
300g Savoy cabbage, shredded·
2 tbsp soya flour
4 eggs

Cook the squash in a pan of boiling water for 12–15 minutes until tender. Drain and return to the pan, mashing together with the spring onions, crème fraîche and seasoning.

Meanwhile, steam the cabbage for 5–6 minutes until tender. If you don't have a steamer, place the cabbage in a colander over a pan of simmering water and cover with a lid to trap in the steam. Add the cabbage to the squash and mix in well. Leave to cool.

When cool enough to handle, shape into four burger-like cakes. Dust the cakes lightly with flour.

Heat 3 drops of oil in a non-stick frying pan and wipe off with kitchen paper. Cook the bubble and squeak cakes for 3–4 minutes each side, until golden.

Meanwhile, bring a frying pan of water to a simmer and gently drop in the 4 eggs. Poach for 5–6 minutes (depending on how well done you like your eggs), then remove with a slotted spoon and keep warm. Serve with the bubble and squeak.

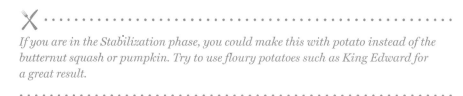

If you are in the Stabilization phase, you could make this with potato instead of the butternut squash or pumpkin. Try to use floury potatoes such as King Edward for a great result.

PUMPKIN RISOTTO

Serves 4 Preparation time: **15 minutes** Cooking time: **40 minutes**

Risotto is a really comforting and filling food, which can be made with such a variety of ingredients and without the mounds of butter that are sometimes used. Try this basic recipe with other ingredients too, such as peas and mint, or mushrooms.

stabilization

1 onion, peeled and diced
1 tbsp chopped fresh sage
175g arborio rice
600ml hot vegetable stock
275g pumpkin or butternut squash, peeled and diced
40g Parmesan cheese, grated

Heat 3 drops of oil in a non-stick saucepan and wipe off with kitchen paper. Sauté the onion for 3–4 minutes until starting to soften.

Add the chopped sage and cook for another 2 minutes.

Stir in the rice, then pour over two ladles of the stock and, stirring continuously, cook until the rice has absorbed the liquid.

Stir in the pumpkin or squash along with another ladle of stock. Continue to cook and stir until the liquid is absorbed again.

Continue to cook this way, adding stock, until the pumpkin is cooked and the rice is *al dente* (tender but with a little bite). The texture should be loose and creamy.

Serve sprinkled with the grated Parmesan.

TOFU-STUFFED CABBAGE

Serves 4 Preparation time: 25 minutes Cooking time: 35 minutes

 cruise pv

consolidation

stabilization

This is a really unusual dish, but well worth the effort. Cabbage leaves are great for using to wrap around ingredients — vary the filling each time you make these, adding your favourite spices or herbs too.

400g leeks, washed, trimmed and
  finely chopped
75g mushrooms, finely diced
400ml vegetable stock
100g tofu, drained and roughly chopped
2 tbsp sesame seeds, toasted

Seasoning
16 leaves from 1 large green cabbage
500g cooked beetroot, grated
1 garlic clove, peeled and crushed
Grated zest of ½ orange
1 tbsp balsamic vinegar

Heat 3 drops of oil in a non-stick pan and wipe off with kitchen paper. Sauté the leeks and mushrooms for 8–10 minutes, stirring occasionally.

Add 100ml of the stock and let the vegetables simmer for 3–4 minutes. Stir in the tofu and sesame seeds. Season well and leave to cool slightly.

Blanch the cabbage leaves in boiling water for 5 minutes, then refresh under running cold water and drain.

Lay two leaves on top of each other, spoon an eighth of the mixture into the centre of the first leaf and roll up to seal before rolling the second leaf around it. Repeat with the remaining mixture and leaves.

Place the parcels, seam side down, in a frying pan, pour over the remaining stock, cover and simmer for 15–18 minutes.

While they are cooking, heat another 3 drops of oil in a non-stick pan and wipe off with kitchen paper. Cook the beetroot with the garlic and orange zest, stir-frying for 5–6 minutes, before stirring in the vinegar and cooking for a further 2–3 minutes.

Serve the cabbage leaves with the beetroot.

VEGETABLE COTTAGE PIE

Serves 4 Preparation time: 15 minutes Cooking time: 35–40 minutes

 *consolidation*

stabilization

A twist on the meaty version, but just as delicious! Use a variety of vegetables depending on the season — parsnips are great in the winter, whilst courgettes and green beans are at their best in summer.

1 onion, peeled and chopped
2 carrots, peeled and diced
2 sticks of celery, diced
50g mushrooms, sliced
2 garlic cloves, peeled and crushed
1 tbsp tomato purée
400g tin green lentils, drained
400g tin chopped tomatoes

2 tsp chopped fresh thyme leaves
100ml vegetable stock
550g butternut squash,
    peeled and chopped
2 tbsp low-fat crème fraîche
Seasoning
75g Manchego cheese, grated

Preheat the oven to 200°C/400° F/Gas 6.

Heat 3 drops of oil in a large non-stick pan and wipe off with kitchen paper. Sauté the onion for 2–3 minutes before adding the carrots, celery, mushrooms and garlic and cooking for a further 2–3 minutes.

Stir in the tomato purée, lentils, chopped tomatoes, thyme and stock and bring to a simmer. Cook for 15 minutes, until the vegetables are tender.

Meanwhile, cook the butternut squash in a pan of boiling water for 10–12 minutes, until tender. Drain the butternut, return to the pan with the crème fraîche and mash until smooth. Season well.

Spoon the lentil mixture into an ovenproof dish and then spread over the butternut topping. Sprinkle with the Manchego cheese and bake in the oven for 15 minutes, until bubbling and golden.

WINTER BEAN & TOFU CASSEROLE

Serves 4 Preparation time: **15 minutes** Cooking time: **1 hour**

Perfect for warming up on a winter's day, this casserole is filling and nutritious.
Vary the type of beans you include depending on what is in your store cupboard.
And if you are not fond of tofu, try adding cooked chicken or prawns instead.

consolidation

stabilization

2 sticks of celery, diced
2 carrots, peeled and diced
2 leeks, washed, trimmed and sliced
1 garlic clove, peeled and crushed
50ml white wine
400g tin chopped tomatoes
400ml vegetable stock

400g tin borlotti beans, drained
   and rinsed
400g tin cannellini beans, drained
   and rinsed
Few fresh oregano leaves, chopped
300g tofu, drained and cut into cubes
Seasoning
Steamed broccoli, to serve

Heat 3 drops of oil in a large non-stick casserole or pan and wipe off with kitchen paper. Cook the celery, carrots and leeks for 8–10 minutes. Add the garlic and wine and let the wine reduce for 3–4 minutes.

Pour in the chopped tomatoes and stock and cook for 15 minutes before adding the beans and oregano and cooking for a further 15 minutes.

Finally, add the tofu and cook for 10 minutes. Season to taste.

Serve in warmed shallow bowls with steamed broccoli.

LENTIL MOUSSAKA

Serves 4 Preparation time: **15 minutes** Cooking time: **45-55 minutes**

A vegetarian version of a classic dish. The usual béchamel and egg topping is replaced with a clever creamy Dukan combination of quark, cream cheese, yoghurt and egg, which I think tastes just as good!

consolidation

stabilization

1 aubergine, cut into thin rounds
1 onion, peeled and chopped
1 red pepper, deseeded and diced
2 garlic cloves, peeled and crushed
50g tomato purée
400g tin chopped tomatoes
400g tin green lentils, drained
100g dried red lentils
100ml vegetable stock

2 tbsp chopped fresh parsley
Seasoning
100g virtually fat-free quark
100g extra-light cream cheese
100g fat-free natural yoghurt
1 egg, beaten
50g pecorino cheese, grated
Steamed green vegetables, to serve

Preheat the oven to 180°C/350°F/Gas 4.

Lay the aubergine slices on a non-stick baking sheet and bake in the oven for 25–30 minutes.

Meanwhile, heat 3 drops of oil in a non-stick pan and wipe off with kitchen paper. Sauté the onion, red pepper and garlic for 2–3 minutes, until starting to soften. Add the tomato purée and cook for a further 1–2 minutes before pouring in the chopped tomatoes, green and red lentils and stock. Cook for 12–14 minutes, until the red lentils swell.

Stir in the parsley, season to taste and pour into an ovenproof dish. Top with the slices of aubergine.

Mix together the quark, cream cheese, yoghurt and egg and spread over the aubergine slices. Sprinkle with the grated pecorino and bake in the oven for 20–25 minutes, until golden brown and bubbling.

Serve with steamed green vegetables.

 . . . .

Aubergines tend to soak up a lot of oil, so baking them this way reduces on the amount of fat you are likely to consume.

. . . .

RATATOUILLE-STUFFED PANCAKES

Serves 4 Preparation time: **30 minutes** Cooking time: **1 hour**

The pancake batter in this recipe can be used with different fillings from the one suggested here — either sweet or savoury — and makes a brilliant and satisfying alternative to other starchy foods in the Consolidation phase.

consolidation

stabilization

110g plain flour
1 tbsp oat bran
2 eggs
300ml skimmed milk
1 large onion, peeled and chopped
1 garlic clove, peeled and crushed
1 red pepper, deseeded and chopped

1 yellow pepper, deseeded and chopped
1 aubergine, cut into 1cm dice
3 medium courgettes, cut into 1cm dice
8 tomatoes, chopped
5–6 fresh basil leaves
1 tbsp tomato purée
100g Gruyère cheese, grated

To make the pancake mix, place the flour and oat bran in a large bowl and whisk in the eggs and milk until smooth. Leave to stand while you make the ratatouille.

Heat 3 drops of oil in a non-stick pan and wipe off with kitchen paper. Sauté the onion for 3–4 minutes before adding the peppers, aubergine and courgette and continuing to cook for 8–10 minutes, stirring from time to time, until the vegetables start to soften.

Stir in the chopped tomatoes, basil, tomato purée and 100ml water. Bring to a simmer and cook for 15–20 minutes.

Preheat the oven to 180°C/350°F/Gas 4.

Meanwhile, cook the pancakes. Heat another 3 drops of oil in a non-stick frying pan and wipe off with kitchen paper. Pour a ladle of the pancake batter into the pan and swirl it around until the surface of the pan is covered. Cook for 2–3 minutes until golden underneath, then flip the pancake and cook for a further 1–2 minutes on the other side.

Slide the pancake onto a piece of greaseproof paper and keep warm while you repeat with the remaining batter.

Lay each pancake on a work surface and place a couple of spoonfuls of the ratatouille on each one. Fold over the sides and roll up the pancake like a spring roll. Place the pancakes into an ovenproof dish, sprinkle with the grated Gruyère, then bake in the oven for 20–25 minutes, until the pancakes are heated through. Serve hot.

POLENTA PIZZA

Serves 2 Preparation time: **20 minutes** Cooking time: **35–40 minutes**

consolidation

stabilization

If you love pizza, this is a really simple way to make a pizza base, which you can top with ingredients of your choice. I really like a pepper topping, and the roasted peppers here could be added without roasting if wished — just deseed and cut into strips.

2 red peppers, halved and deseeded
1 yellow pepper, halved and deseeded
125g polenta
Seasoning
½ tsp dried oregano
200g tin chopped tomatoes
5–6 fresh basil leaves, roughly torn
30g Cheddar cheese, grated

Preheat the oven to 200°C/400°F/Gas 6. Use 3 drops of oil to grease a baking sheet lightly and wipe off with kitchen paper.

Place the peppers under a hot grill, skin side up, and cook until blackened. Place in a bowl, cover with cling film and leave to cool.

Meanwhile, bring 500ml water to the boil in a saucepan. Slowly pour in the polenta, stirring constantly. Add seasoning and the dried oregano and continue to cook, stirring, for 8–10 minutes, until the polenta is thick.

Pour the polenta out onto the lightly oiled baking sheet and spread into a circle. Bake in the oven for 12 minutes.

Remove the cling film from the bowl of peppers and peel off the charred skins. Roughly slice the roast peppers.

Take the polenta out of the oven and spread the chopped tomatoes over it. Top with the roast peppers and torn basil leaves, then sprinkle with the grated cheese. Bake for another 12–15 minutes, until the cheese is golden and bubbling.

Serve hot, cut into wedges.

PEPPER & COURGETTE LASAGNE

Serves 4 Preparation time: 25 minutes Cooking time: 1 hour

Lasagne is another family favourite and this recipe is perfect for the vegetarian in the family, but can be enjoyed by everyone.

consolidation

stabilization

1 red onion, peeled and sliced
2 garlic cloves, peeled and crushed
2 red peppers, deseeded and finely
  chopped
1 yellow pepper, deseeded and finely
  chopped
450g courgettes, sliced

2 tsp chopped fresh thyme
2 x 400g tins chopped tomatoes
8 sheets wholewheat lasagne
300g extra-light cream cheese
75ml skimmed milk
50g Parmesan cheese, grated

Preheat the oven to 180°C/350°F/Gas 4.

Heat 3 drops of oil in a large non-stick pan and wipe off with kitchen paper. Fry the onion and garlic for 2–3 minutes. Add the peppers and courgettes and continue to cook for 6–8 minutes, until the vegetables start to soften.

Stir in the thyme and tomatoes and cook for 10–12 minutes.

Whisk together the cream cheese and milk.

Spoon half the vegetable mixture into the bottom of an ovenproof dish, then top with 4 of the lasagne sheets and half of the cheese sauce. Repeat with the remaining vegetables, lasagne and cheese sauce, then sprinkle with the grated Parmesan.

Bake for 1 hour until golden and bubbling, then serve.

VEGETABLE MASALA

Serves 4 Preparation time: 20 minutes Cooking time: 40-45 minutes

cruise pv

consolidation

stabilization

Vegetable curry is such a filling, satisfying meal and you can vary the vegetables to suit what you have or prefer.

1 tsp cumin seeds
1 tsp mustard seeds
1 onion, peeled and chopped
2 garlic cloves, peeled and sliced
2cm piece fresh root ginger, peeled
   and finely chopped
200g carrots, peeled and chopped

200g butternut squash, peeled
   and chopped
½ small cauliflower, broken into florets
2 tsp garam masala
400g tin chopped tomatoes
200g baby spinach leaves
2 tbsp chopped fresh coriander
Natural yoghurt, to serve

Heat 3 drops of oil in a non-stick frying pan and wipe off with kitchen paper. Cook the cumin seeds and mustard seeds for 1–2 minutes, until the mustard seeds begin to 'pop'.

Add the onion, garlic and ginger and cook for 3–4 minutes. Stir in the carrots, butternut squash, cauliflower and garam masala, then pour in the chopped tomatoes and mix well.

Bring to a simmer, cover and cook for 25–30 minutes, stirring occasionally.

Stir in the spinach and cook for a further 3–4 minutes, uncovered.

Sprinkle in the chopped coriander and serve with natural yoghurt.

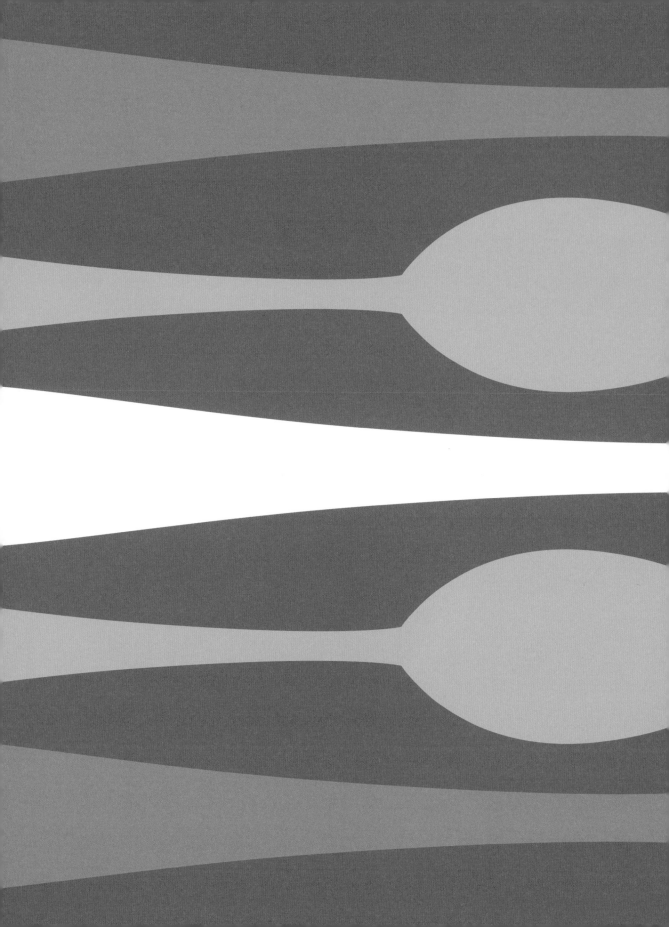

FRIENDS FOR DINNER

SEARED SCALLOPS
WITH PEA PURÉE & HAM

Serves 4 Preparation time: **5 minutes** Cooking time: **10 minutes**

cruise pv

consolidation

stabilization

I think scallops always look so impressive for a dinner party and this recipe is very simple to make. Scallops are easily cleaned just by washing in cold water. If you wish you can remove the coral, which is the roe of the scallop, but it does taste delicious so give it a try before you decide!

300g fresh or frozen peas
6–8 fresh mint leaves
Seasoning
12 scallops, cleaned
2 tbsp fat-free natural yoghurt
150g lean ham, sliced

Bring a small pan of water to the boil and cook the peas, mint and seasoning for about 5 minutes.

Meanwhile, heat 3 drops of oil in a non-stick frying pan and wipe off with kitchen paper. Cook the scallops for 2–3 minutes on each side, until golden and cooked though. Do not overcook or the scallops will become tough.

Drain the peas, stir in the yoghurt and purée with a hand blender until smooth. If you don't have a hand blender, you can use a fork for a more rustic feel.

Divide the slices of ham among four warmed plates and top with the pea purée and golden scallops.

ASPARAGUS
WITH POACHED EGG

Serves 4 Preparation time: **5 minutes** Cooking time: **10-15 minutes**

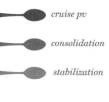

cruise pv

consolidation

stabilization

I love asparagus and this is one of the simplest recipes in the book, but it is just perfect in the spring when asparagus comes into season and is full of flavour. Asparagus can be steamed or boiled and really doesn't need to cook for long as it's also possible to eat it raw.

4 eggs
2 bunches asparagus, woody ends removed
2 tsp chopped fresh tarragon
Seasoning

Bring a frying pan of water to a simmer and gently drop in the 4 eggs. Poach for 5–6 minutes (depending on how well done you like your eggs), then remove with a slotted spoon and keep warm.

Bring a large pan of water to the boil and cook or steam the asparagus for 2–3 minutes, until tender.

Toss the asparagus with the chopped tarragon, then divide among four warmed plates.

Top the asparagus with the poached eggs, then add seasoning and serve.

If you are not in the Cruise phase, you could sprinkle 25g Parmesan shavings over the asparagus and poached eggs.

CHICKEN & HERB SOUFFLÉ

Serves 4   Preparation time: **10 minutes**   Cooking time: **45 minutes**

Soufflés are much easier than most people think and are an impressive and delicious starter to serve at a dinner party. Be brave and try this recipe the next time you have friends for dinner — they will never guess you are on a diet!

consolidation

stabilization

½ tbsp vegetable oil
3 shallots, peeled and finely diced
2 tbsp wholemeal flour
100ml chicken stock
150ml skimmed milk
4 skinless cooked chicken breasts, shredded

1 tbsp chopped fresh tarragon
6 tbsp low-fat crème fraîche
Seasoning
4 eggs, separated
1 tbsp grated Parmesan cheese

Preheat the oven to 200°C/400°F/Gas 6. Use 3 drops of oil to grease a large soufflé dish lightly and wipe off with kitchen paper.

Heat the oil in a pan and sauté the shallots until transparent. Stir in the flour and continue to cook for 2–3 minutes. Gradually pour in the chicken stock and skimmed milk and bring to a simmer. Cook, stirring, for 3–4 minutes, until smooth and creamy.

Stir in the chicken breast, tarragon and crème fraîche and season well. Stir the egg yolks into the sauce.

Place the egg whites into a grease-free bowl and whisk until very stiff, and then carefully fold into the chicken mixture with the grated Parmesan.

Spoon into the prepared dish and bakein the oven for 30 minutes, until slightly risen and golden. Serve immediately.

CHICKEN CAESAR SALAD

Serves 4 Preparation time: **14 minutes** Cooking time: **10-12 minutes**

This is a traditional recipe that is loved by all, and you can vary your protein — make it with chicken, turkey, prawns, salmon or even steak, if you wish. When you are in the Consolidation phase, you can add Parmesan; I find that using a vegetable peeler is the perfect way to make Parmesan shavings.

cruise pv

consolidation

stabilization

2 skinless chicken breasts
3 rashers light bacon
10g tinned anchovy fillets
1 tsp capers, drained
1 tsp Worcestershire sauce
½ tsp Dijon mustard

Juice of ½ lemon
½ garlic clove, peeled and crushed
1 egg, boiled for 1½ minutes only
1 tsp olive oil
2 cos lettuces

Heat 3 drops of oil in a griddle pan and wipe off with kitchen paper. Heat until really hot and cook the chicken breasts for 4–5 minutes on each side, until cooked through. Check that they are cooked by poking with the tip of a sharp knife — there should be no sign of pink and the juices will run clear. Remove from the griddle and leave to rest for 2–3 minutes before cutting into thin slices.

Place the bacon onto the griddle and cook until crisp. Remove from the griddle, then roughly chop.

For the dressing, place the anchovy fillets, capers, Worcestershire sauce, mustard, lemon juice, garlic, egg and olive oil in a blender and blend until smooth, adding a little water to loosen if needed.

Roughly tear the leaves of the lettuce and place in a large bowl with the chicken and bacon. Toss the dressing into the salad until everything is coated and serve.

✗ ·

If you are in the Stabilization or Consolidation phases, you can add 1 tablespoon grated Parmesan cheese to the dressing and top the salad with a few tablespoons of Parmesan shavings. You could also include croûtons to make this even more delicious. Cut 2 thick slices of wholemeal bread into 2cm cubes and toast them under a hot grill for 1-2 minutes, tossing a few times, until golden.

· ·

SALMON & BROCCOLI TABBOULEH

Serves 4 Preparation time: **10 minutes** Cooking time: **15 minutes**

The couscous in this recipe could be substituted with bulgur wheat, quinoa or brown rice, if you prefer. Add lots of herbs to give it real depth of flavour.

consolidation

stabilization

200g couscous
200g broccoli florets
Large handful of fresh parsley, chopped
Large handful of fresh mint, chopped
8 spring onions, sliced
Grated zest of ½ lime
Seasoning
4 x 150g salmon fillets

Place the couscous in a bowl, pour over enough boiling water just to cover and leave to stand for 10 minutes.

Meanwhile, steam the broccoli over boiling water, then refresh under running cold water. If you don't have a steamer, place the broccoli in a colander over a pan of simmering water and cover with a lid to trap in the steam. Alternatively you can blanch the broccoli.

Fluff the couscous with a fork, then stir in the chopped herbs, spring onions, lime zest, broccoli and seasoning.

Grill the salmon fillets for 3–4 minutes on each side and serve with the couscous. Alternatively, you could flake the fish and stir into the tabbouleh to serve.

ROASTED MONKFISH
WITH CELERIAC COLESLAW

Serves 4 Preparation time: 18 minutes Cooking time: 15 minutes

cruise pv

consolidation

stabilization

I love this celeriac coleslaw and now prefer it to the cabbage version. Monkfish is a thick, meaty fish that has a transparent membrane covering its flesh. This is hard to remove, so ask your fishmonger if he could do it for you.

2 x 350g thick pieces of monkfish fillet
Seasoning
1 tsp cumin seeds
1 small celeriac, peeled
Juice of ½ lemon

2 medium carrots, peeled and
  coarsely grated
4 tbsp fat-free natural yoghurt
2 tsp Dijon mustard
1 tbsp chopped fresh parsley

Preheat the oven to 200°C/400°F/Gas 6.

Heat 3 drops of oil in a non-stick ovenproof frying pan and wipe off with kitchen paper. Season the monkfish and sear for 3–4 minutes until nicely browned on all sides. Transfer the pan to the oven and roast for 10–12 minutes, until the fish is cooked through but still moist in the centre. Remove from the oven, cover in foil and set aside for 5 minutes.

Toast the cumin seeds in a dry frying pan for 1–2 minutes, until the aroma starts to fill the room.

Cut the celeriac into long matchsticks as thin as you can and place in a bowl with the lemon juice and cumin seeds.

Stir in the grated carrot, yoghurt, mustard and parsley and season to taste.

Serve the monkfish cut into thick slices on a bed of celeriac coleslaw.

✕ •

If you are in the Consolidation phase, you can add a Granny Smith apple to the coleslaw, cut into long matchsticks.

• •

SMOKED HADDOCK & SPRING ONION RISOTTO

Serves 4 Preparation time: **15 minutes** Cooking time: **35 minutes**

stabilization

Normally making risotto is very time-consuming, taking you away from your dinner guests, but I love this version as it can be cooked in the oven and is great served with a simple crisp green salad.

6 spring onions, thickly sliced
1 garlic clove, peeled and crushed
300g arborio rice
600ml vegetable stock
350ml skimmed milk

325g skinless smoked haddock fillets
2 tbsp low-fat crème fraîche
Juice of ½ lemon
10g Parmesan cheese, grated

Preheat the oven to 200°C/400°F/Gas 6.

Heat 3 drops of oil in a non-stick ovenproof pan and wipe off with kitchen paper. Sauté the spring onions for 6–7 minutes, until softening and starting to turn golden.

Add the garlic and rice and stir whilst cooking for another 2 minutes.

Pour in the stock and milk and bring to the boil, then simmer for 10 minutes.

Place the haddock on top of the risotto, cover with foil and bake in the oven for 15 minutes, until the rice is tender and the haddock is cooked through.

Remove from the oven and stir in the crème fraîche and lemon juice, gently breaking up and stirring in the haddock at the same time.

Serve sprinkled with the grated Parmesan.

SALMON CEVICHE

Serves 4 Preparation time: **1 hour**

What could be easier that this — no cooking involved at all! A great Mexican dish that can be made with most fresh fish.

500g skinless salmon fillet
Juice of 3 limes
1 shallot, peeled and finely diced
1 tsp black pepper
Handful of fresh coriander, chopped

Thinly slice the salmon and place in a shallow non-metallic bowl.

Mix together the lime juice and shallot and season with black pepper.

Pour the lime juice over the fish. Cover and place in the fridge for 50 minutes, stirring gently after 25 minutes.

Remove from the fridge 5 minutes before eating to allow the flavours to develop.

Spoon onto plates and sprinkle with the chopped coriander to serve.

attack
cruise
consolidation
stabilization

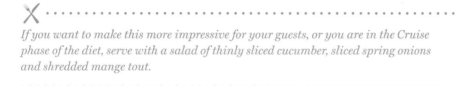

If you want to make this more impressive for your guests, or you are in the Cruise phase of the diet, serve with a salad of thinly sliced cucumber, sliced spring onions and shredded mange tout.

CRAB, TOMATO & SAFFRON TART

Serves 4 Preparation time: **15 minutes** Cooking time: **20-25 minutes**

This is a real summer treat, when crab is in season. Use a mixture of white and dark crabmeat for a really intense flavour. I love crab and buying it fresh from the seaside has to be one of the greatest British treats.

consolidation

stabilization

125g polenta
Pinch of saffron
Seasoning
3 tomatoes, sliced
250g crabmeat (white and dark)
50g reduced-fat Emmental cheese, grated
Crisp green salad, to serve

Preheat the oven to 200°C/400°F/Gas 6. Use 3 drops of oil to grease a 25cm flan tin lightly and wipe off with kitchen paper.

Bring 500ml water to the boil in a saucepan. Slowly pour in the polenta, stirring constantly. Add the saffron and seasoning and continue to cook, stirring, for 8-10 minutes, until the polenta is thick.

Pour out into the flan tin and spread evenly over the base. Top with the sliced tomatoes, then the crabmeat and finally the grated cheese. Bake in the oven for 12-15 minutes, until the cheese is bubbling and golden.

Serve cut into wedges with a crisp green salad.

SPINACH-STUFFED SOLE

Serves 4 Preparation time: 15 minutes Cooking time: 10-15 minutes

cruise pv

consolidation

stabilization

Stuffing fish fillets is really not that difficult and is a great way to add flavour to a simple dish. I think trying new ways of cooking and searching out ingredients you might not usually think of buying helps to make the early stages of the diet enjoyable. And it's easy to serve with a bowl of new potatoes for anyone not on the Dukan.

200g baby spinach leaves
Grated zest of 1 lemon
Seasoning
4 sole fillets

½ tbsp chopped fresh tarragon
50ml white wine
225g broccoli florets

Preheat the oven to 200°C/400°F/Gas 6. Use 3 drops of oil to grease an ovenproof dish lightly and wipe off with kitchen paper.

Wash the baby spinach leaves, then place in a pan with just the residual water and the lemon zest, cover the pan and cook for 2–3 minutes until the spinach has wilted. Drain well in a sieve, squeezing out the excess moisture with the back of a spoon. Season well.

Lay the sole fillets on a work surface and place a quarter of the spinach across the middle of each fillet, top with the tarragon and roll up to enclose the spinach. Season well.

Place the rolled fillets, seam side down, in the ovenproof dish. Pour over the white wine and bake for 8–10 minutes — the fish should be opaque throughout when tested with the tip of a knife.

Meanwhile, cook the broccoli in simmering water until tender.

Serve the spinach-stuffed sole with the broccoli and with any juices from the dish spooned over.

To enjoy this dish in the Attack phase, just sprinkle fish fillets with your favourite herbs and chopped spring onions and cook in the same way, finishing off with a squeeze of lemon juice instead of the wine.

VENISON BURGERS

Serves 4 Preparation time: **15 minutes** Cooking time: **20 minutes**

Everyone loves a burger, and these are a real treat. Using tasty venison meat gives a rich flavour and the burger is much healthier without the bun! Ask your butcher for the best mince.

cruise pv

consolidation

stabilization

1 small onion, peeled and finely chopped
1 garlic clove, peeled and finely chopped
500g minced venison
1½ tbsp oat bran
1 egg, beaten
1 tsp Dijon mustard
1 tsp Worcestershire sauce

1 tsp tomato purée
2 tbsp chopped fresh parsley
4 tomatoes, diced
1 small red onion, peeled and diced
1 tsp red wine vinegar
Salad leaves, to serve

Heat 3 drops of oil in a non-stick frying pan and wipe off with kitchen paper. Sauté the onion and garlic for 3–4 minutes.

Place the minced venison in a large bowl and mix together with the oat bran, egg, mustard, Worcestershire sauce, ketchup and half the parsley.

Add the onion and garlic and mix well.

Using wet hands, shape the mixture into four burgers.

Heat another lightly oiled pan and cook the burgers for 7–8 minutes on each side, until cooked through.

Meanwhile, mix together the remaining parsley with the chopped tomatoes, red onion and red wine vinegar.

Serve the burgers on a bed of salad leaves, topped with the tomato and red onion salad.

✗ ·

To enjoy these burgers in the Attack phase, just omit the salad leaves and tomatoes.

· ·

SESAME-SEARED TUNA
WITH CUCUMBER SALAD

Serves 2 Preparation time: 10 minutes + 10 minutes marinating Cooking time: 4-6 minutes

cruise pv

consolidation

stabilization

Tuna is a very meaty fish and I think it is a really tasty and satisfying ingredient to fill you up in the early stages of the diet. Searing tuna in a hot pan prevents it from becoming tough with overcooking.

2 x 150g tuna steaks
2 tbsp soy sauce
⅓ cucumber, cut into matchsticks
3 spring onions, shredded
2 tbsp sesame seeds
Juice of 1 lime

Place the tuna in a non-metallic bowl with the soy sauce and leave to stand for 10 minutes, turning once.

Meanwhile, mix together the cucumber and spring onions.

Roll the tuna in the sesame seeds, then cook in a hot pan for 2–3 minutes on each side (the inside should still be pink). Leave to rest for 2 minutes before slicing thinly and serving on the cucumber salad, sprinkled with lime juice.

You can have tuna in the Attack phase, without the cucumber salad but with just a little soy sauce for dipping.

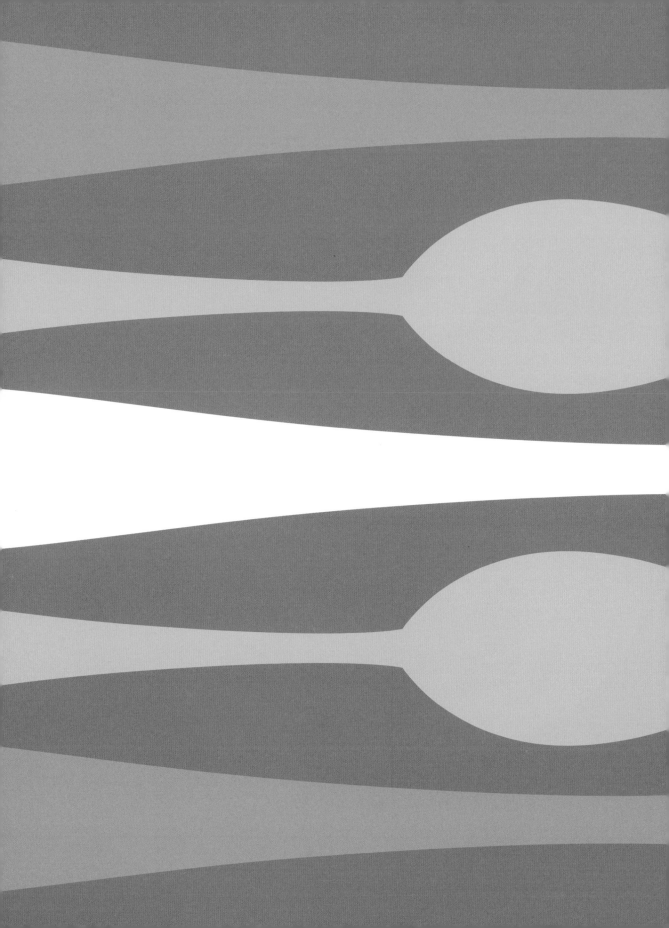

DESSERTS

ETON MESS

Serves 4 Preparation time: **15 minutes** Cooking time: **30–40 minutes**

A traditional summer dessert, best eaten when strawberries are in season,
but raspberries also work just as well. It's one of my favourite summer recipes.

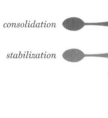

consolidation

stabilization

1 egg white
½ tsp cornflour
3 tbsp sweetener
75g strawberries, hulled and chopped
200g fat-free natural yoghurt

Preheat the oven to 150°C/300°F/Gas 2. Line a baking sheet with greaseproof paper.

Whisk the egg white until stiff, and then whisk in the cornflour and sweetener until thick and glossy.

Place the mixture onto the prepared baking sheet in two large spoonfuls. Bake in the oven for 30–40 minutes, until crisp. Remove from the oven and allow to cool.

Break up the meringue, mix with the strawberries and yoghurt and spoon into four small glasses to serve.

In the Cruise phase you could add strawberry flavouring (visit mydukandietshop.co.uk)
to the yoghurt instead of the chopped strawberries.

OAT BRAN PANCAKES
WITH RASPBERRY PURÉE

Serves 4 Preparation time: 10 minutes Cooking time: 30–40 minutes

stabilization

You can use this really useful basic pancake recipe for other sweet or savoury dishes and can adjust the amount of flour versus oat bran to suit you. As long as your mixture looks the consistency of double cream, your pancakes will work.

110g plain flour
1 tbsp oat bran
2 eggs
300ml skimmed milk
350g raspberries
Sweetener (optional)
4 tbsp fat-free Greek yoghurt and freshly grated nutmeg, to serve

Place the flour and oat bran in a large bowl and gradually whisk in the eggs and milk until you have a smooth batter the consistency of double cream. Leave to stand for a few minutes.

Purée the raspberries in a blender or food processor or even with a potato masher. Push through a sieve to get rid of the small pips. Stir in a little sweetener to taste, if you wish.

Heat 3 drops of oil in a non-stick frying pan and wipe off with kitchen paper. Pour a ladle of the pancake batter into the pan and swirl it around until the surface of the pan is covered. Cook for 2–3 minutes until golden underneath, then flip the pancake and cook for a further 1–2 minutes on the other side.

Slide the pancake onto a piece of greaseproof paper and keep warm while you repeat with the remaining batter.

Spoon a little raspberry purée over each pancake, fold in quarters, then serve two to three per person, topped with a dollop of yoghurt and a sprinkling of freshly grated nutmeg.

BAKED SPICED
PASSION FRUIT PLUMS

Serves 4 Preparation time: **15 minutes** Cooking time: **30 minutes**

A perfect way to cook seasonal ripe plums — they are at their best in autumn, so the need for extra sweetness is not required. If you have a Victoria plum tree in your garden, this is the perfect way to use them!

stabilization

400g ripe plums, stoned and cut into quarters
1 tsp ground cinnamon
4 passion fruits
1 tbsp sweetener
1 tbsp flaked almonds, toasted

Preheat the oven to 170°C/325°F/Gas 3.

Place the plums into a roasting tray and sprinkle with 1 tablespoon water and the ground cinnamon. Bake in the oven for 30 minutes, until soft. Remove the plums with a slotted spoon and arrange in four shallow bowls.

Meanwhile, halve the passion fruits and spoon the insides into a sieve placed over a bowl to remove the pips. Push the juices through with the back of a spoon.

Stir the sweetener into the passion fruit juice, mix with the juices from the roast plums, and then spoon over the plums.

Sprinkle with flaked almonds to serve.

✗ . . . .

To serve this as a Consolidation recipe, just omit the flaked almonds.

. . . .

SPICED RHUBARB COMPOTE
WITH ORANGE CREAM

Serves 4 Preparation time: 15 minutes Cooking time: 10 minutes

cruise pv

consolidation

stabilization

A delicious way to serve rhubarb — this great fruit has an affinity with ginger and is wonderful accompanied by a tangy orange cream. It is also officially a vegetable, so you can enjoy this dessert in the Cruise phase.

50g fresh root ginger, peeled and grated
3 tbsp sweetener
300g rhubarb, trimmed and cut into 1–2 cm pieces
3 tbsp fat-free Greek yoghurt
3 tbsp low-fat crème fraîche
Grated zest of 1 orange

Place the ginger and sweetener in a pan with 150ml water and bring to the boil, then simmer for 2–3 minutes.

Stir in the rhubarb and simmer for 4–5 minutes. Remove from the heat, cover the pan and leave to cool, stirring from time to time.

Meanwhile, beat together the yoghurt, crème fraîche and orange zest.

Serve the gingered rhubarb compote with a big dollop of orange cream.

MANGO MOUSSE

Serves 4 Preparation time: 15 minutes + chilling Cooking time: 3-4 minutes

A really light and fluffy mousse, perfect for a summer's day. If you are in the Consolidation phase, top with fresh raspberries to serve, but if you are in the Stabilization phase, you can sprinkle with chopped pistachio nuts.

consolidation

stabilization

2 leaves of gelatine
2 mangoes, stoned, peeled and chopped
Grated zest and juice of ½ lime
2 egg whites
2 tbsp low-fat crème fraîche
2 tbsp chopped pistachio nuts or a few raspberries, to serve

Soak the gelatine leaves in a small bowl of water.

Place the chopped mangoes into a food processor or blender and blend until smooth.

Place the mango purée in a small pan and heat gently with the drained and squeezed gelatine leaves, stirring constantly until the leaves have dissolved. Remove from the heat and stir in the lime zest and juice.

In a grease-free bowl, whisk the egg whites until stiff.

Fold the egg whites and crème fraîche into the mango purée mixture. Divide among four small glasses or bowls and place in the fridge to chill for at least 30 minutes.

Serve sprinkled with chopped pistachios or fresh raspberries.

 . . . .

Those who might be at risk from the effects of salmonella food poisoning should be careful about eating raw or lightly cooked eggs.

. . . .

CHOCOLATE ICE CREAM

Serves 4 Preparation time: **10 minutes + freezing**

cruise

consolidation

stabilization

Fat-free ice cream will never have the same soft texture as normal ice cream, so be prepared to leave it to soften a little before serving, by transferring it to the fridge 20 minutes beforehand. A delicious accompaniment to oranges if you're at the consolidation stage.

400g tofu, drained
3 tbsp fat-reduced, sugar-free cocoa powder
2 tbsp sweetener
2 tbsp low-fat crème fraîche

Place all the ingredients in a food processor or blender and blend until totally smooth. Taste for sweetness.

Pour into a freezerproof container with a lid and place in the freezer.

After 1 hour, take out and whisk with a fork to break up the ice crystals. Do this again after another 45 minutes. Leave to freeze for another hour before serving.

STRAWBERRY SHORTCAKE

Serves 4 Preparation time: **10 minutes** Cooking time: **30 minutes**

consolidation

stabilization

Strawberries are my favourite fruit and this recipe just reminds me how good they can be. A twist on the American classic — enjoy this oat bran version when strawberries are at their best.

8 tbsp oat bran
90g fat-free natural yoghurt
2 eggs, beaten
4–6 tsp sweetener

2 lemons
300g fat-free Greek yoghurt
250g strawberries, hulled and sliced

Mix together the oat bran, natural yoghurt, eggs and sweetener. Grate the zest of 1 of the lemons and add to the mixture.

Heat 3 drops of oil in a small non-stick frying pan and wipe off with kitchen paper. Spoon half the mixture into the pan. Spread the mixture around until you have a circle of about 18cm. Cook for 8–10 minutes, until the batter sets and is golden underneath.

Turn over and cook for another 4–5 minutes until golden on the other side. Remove from the pan and leave to cool on a wire rack.

Repeat with the remaining batter.

Cut each cooked round into six wedges. Stack three wedges on each plate with the Greek yoghurt and strawberries in between each layer.

Thinly pare the zest of the remaining lemon and cut into fine strips. Sprinkle the shortcake with the strips of lemon zest to serve.

PLUM PUDDING

Serves 4 Preparation time: **5 minutes** Cooking time: **30 minutes**

These delicious little puddings can be served at Christmas time to replace Christmas pudding — the spices and fruit are a perfect substitute and they makes a very festive Dukan alternative.

consolidation

stabilization

6 ripe plums, stoned and chopped
25g goji berries
1 tsp sweetener
½ tsp ground cinnamon

1 tsp ground mixed spice
4 tbsp oat bran
150g fat-free natural yoghurt and
    ¼ tsp grated nutmeg, to serve

Preheat the oven to 200°C/400°F/Gas 6.

Place the plums, goji berries, 1 tablespoon water and the sweetener in a small pan and simmer for 10–12 minutes, until very soft.

Stir in the spices and oat bran and spoon into four ramekin dishes. Bake in the oven for 15 minutes.

Leave to stand for 2–3 minutes, then turn out onto four plates and serve each with a dollop of natural yoghurt sprinkled with grated nutmeg.

RHUBARB & GINGER SORBET

Serves 4 Preparation time: 10 minutes + cooling and freezing Cooking time: 15 minutes

cruise pv

consolidation

stabilization

Sorbets are very refreshing and are a perfect treat on a summer's day. The great thing about using rhubarb in a recipe is that it is actually a vegetable, not a fruit, so can be eaten in the Cruise phase.

400g rhubarb, cut into 1cm pieces
15g sweetener
1cm piece fresh root ginger, peeled and grated
2 egg whites

Place the rhubarb in a pan with 1 tablespoon of water, half the sweetener and the ginger. Cover and cook over a low heat for 12–15 minutes, until completely soft. Leave to cool for 10 minutes.

Place in a food processor or blender and blend to a smooth purée.

Whisk the egg whites with the remaining sweetener until stiff peaks are formed.

Fold the rhubarb into the egg whites, making sure it is all incorporated.

Spoon into a freezable container and place in the freezer. After about 1 hour, take out and break up with a fork, then replace and freeze until needed.

The sorbet may need to be taken out of the freezer and placed in the fridge 20–30 minutes before serving to soften slightly.

 ·

Those who might be at risk from the effects of salmonella food poisoning should be careful about eating raw or lightly cooked eggs.

· ·

KIWI BRÛLÉE

Serves 4 Preparation time: **15 minutes** Cooking time: **2–3 minutes**

Kiwis are a great source of vitamin C and taste delicious in this creamy recipe.
You could also use other fruits — mangoes and raspberries work really well.

consolidation

stabilization

3 tbsp oat bran
8 tbsp fat-free Greek yoghurt
8 tbsp low-fat crème fraîche
Grated zest of 1 lime
4 kiwi fruits, peeled and chopped
¼ tsp ground cinnamon
2 tsp sweetener

Toast the oat bran by cooking for 2–3 minutes in a small pan over a medium heat —
keep an eye on it and, once it is brown, take it off the heat and pour into a bowl.

Beat together the Greek yoghurt and crème fraîche with the lime zest.

Place the chopped kiwi fruit in the bottom of four ramekin dishes. Spoon over the
creamy yoghurt and crème fraîche, smoothing the top.

Stir the ground cinnamon and sweetener into the toasted oat bran and sprinkle this
over each ramekin before serving.

If you are still in the Attack or Cruise phases, omit the kiwi in the base of this dessert
and, for Attack, swap the crème fraîche with fat-free fromage frais. The topping and
creamy filling are still delicious on their own without the fruit.

SPICED PUMPKIN MOUSSE

Serves 4 Preparation time: 15 minutes + cooling and chilling Cooking time: 10–12 minutes

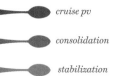

cruise pv

consolidation

stabilization

If you have fresh pumpkin, you can roast this and purée it or you can buy puréed pumpkin in a tin which is obviously much easier.

300ml skimmed milk
1 egg yolk
1 tbsp cornflour
400g tin puréed pumpkin
½ tsp ground cinnamon

½ tsp ground nutmeg, plus extra to serve
½ tsp ground ginger
2–3 tsp sweetener, to taste
3 tbsp low-fat crème fraîche

Place the milk in a small pan and bring to a simmer.

Whisk together the egg yolk and cornflour and pour over the hot milk, whisking continuously.

Pour the mixture back into the pan and cook for 2–3 minutes before adding the pumpkin purée and spices.

Cook for 3–4 minutes, then remove from the heat and leave to cool for 8–10 minutes.

Stir in the sweetener to taste and fold in 2 tablespoons of the crème fraîche. Spoon into four individual glasses or bowls and chill until ready to serve.

Serve with a small dollop of the remaining crème fraîche and a sprinkling of freshly grated nutmeg.

CINNAMON BAKED EGG CUSTARD

Serves 4 Preparation time: **15 minutes** Cooking time: **35–40 minutes**

A real family favourite, cooked by mothers and grandmothers for years, and one you don't need to miss out on at any stage of the diet!

600ml skimmed milk
3 eggs
3–4 tsp sweetener
¼ tsp ground cinnamon
2 tbsp fat-free Greek yoghurt
Freshly grated nutmeg, for topping

Preheat the oven to 150°C/300°F/Gas 2.

Heat the milk in a small pan until hot, but not boiling. Remove from the heat.

In a large bowl, whisk together the eggs, sweetener, cinnamon and yoghurt until smooth. Pour the warmed milk over the egg mixture, whisking continuously, then strain through a sieve.

Place four small ovenproof dishes or cups into a roasting tray and pour the egg mixture into each one. Sprinkle with grated nutmeg. Pour hot water into the tray around the dishes or cups, enough to come halfway up them.

Bake in the oven for 35–40 minutes until set. Cool slightly in the tin and serve warm or cold.

attack
cruise
consolidation
stabilization

✗ . . . .

Looks really pretty topped with pomegranate seeds if you are in the Consolidation phase.

. . . .

CITRUS BAKED APPLES

Serves 4 Preparation time: **15 minutes** Cooking time: **35-40 minutes**

*Sometimes I really want something sweet to finish off a meal and this recipe is perfect.
It is also delicious made with pears or a mixture of both apples and pears.*

consolidation

stabilization

4 apples, peeled, cored and cut into quarters
1 cinnamon stick, broken into 3 pieces
Pinch of grated nutmeg
1 lemon
1 orange
Low-fat crème fraîche, to serve

Preheat the oven to 180°C/350°F/Gas 4.

Place the apple quarters in an ovenproof dish with the cinnamon stick and nutmeg.

Thinly peel the lemon and orange with a vegetable peeler and then cut the zest
into julienne (very fine) strips. Juice the lemon and orange, pour the juice over the
apples and scatter with the citrus zest.

Cover the dish with foil and bake in the oven for 35–40 minutes, until the apples are
just soft.

Serve warm with crème fraîche.

STUFFED PEACHES

Serves 4 Preparation time: **15 minutes** Cooking time: **15 minutes**

consolidation

stabilization

Make use of seasonal fruit as much as you can on the diet. The sweeter the fruit is naturally, the less sweetness you'll need to add. You can also use nectarines or apricots for this recipe if wished.

4 ripe peaches, halved and stoned
2 tbsp oat bran
1 orange
125g extra-light cream cheese
1 tbsp sweetener

Preheat the oven to 180°C/350°F/Gas 4. Place the peaches, cut side up, in an ovenproof dish.

Toast the oat bran in a small pan until it is dark golden. Leave to cool.

Grate the zest of the orange and then peel and segment the fruit (see tip below).

Mix together the oat bran, orange zest, cream cheese and sweetener and spoon the mixture into the dips of the peaches (where the stones have been removed).

Spoon over the orange segments and any juice and bake in the oven for 15 minutes. Serve warm.

 . . . .

To segment an orange, place the orange on a chopping board and cut 1cm off the top and bottom of the fruit. Using a sharp knife, cut down the side of the orange, just deeply enough to remove the peel and the white pith. Then holding the orange, cut down the side of each segment, towards the middle of the fruit, and each segment will drop out. Segment over a bowl to catch the juice.

. . . .

BLACKBERRY FOOL

Serves 4 Preparation time: **15 minutes** + chilling

Try this with other fruits such as raspberries or strawberries. The tofu adds a great texture, but if you like your fool a little smoother, you can just add more Greek yoghurt. No need for lots of cream here!

consolidation

stabilization

250g blackberries
200g tofu, drained
1½ tbsp sweetener
150g fat-free Greek yoghurt

Place the blackberries into a small blender and blend until smooth. Remove half of the blackberry purée and reserve, then add the tofu and sweetener to the blender and blend until smooth again. Finally, add the yoghurt and blend until smooth once more.

Using a spoon, stir the reserved blackberry purée through the mixture, not completely combining it, to give a marbled effect.

Spoon into four glasses or small bowls and chill for a few minutes before serving.

CARDAMOM RICE PUDDING
WITH ROASTED PLUMS

Serves 4 Preparation time: **15 minutes** Cooking time: **2 hours**

stabilization

Rice pudding is a real winter comfort food, and just because you are trying to loose weight, doesn't mean you can't have it.

100g pudding rice
3 tbsp sweetener
700ml semi-skimmed milk
Seeds from 6 cardamom pods, crushed
Strip of lemon zest
8 plums, halved and stoned

Preheat the oven to 130°C/250°F/Gas 1.

Wash the rice and drain well, then tip into an 850ml ovenproof baking dish with 2 tablespoons of the sweetener and stir through the milk.

Sprinkle in the crushed cardamom seeds and stir in with the lemon zest.

Cook in the oven for 2 hours, or until the pudding is thick and creamy.

Meanwhile, place the plums in a roasting tray, sprinkle with the remaining sweetener and roast alongside the rice pudding for 1 hour.

Serve the rice pudding with the roasted plums.

BAKING

SCONES

Serves 4 Preparation time: 15 minutes Cooking time: 8-10 minutes

cruise

consolidation

stabilization

Oat bran and cornflour are used here to make scones — perfect for a summer day in the garden.

5 tbsp oat bran
100g cornflour
½ tbsp sweetener
65g skimmed milk powder

1 egg, beaten
1 tbsp fat-free natural yoghurt
Grated zest of 1 lemon
2 tbsp fat-free Greek yoghurt

Preheat the oven to 200°C/400°F/Gas 6.

Place the oat bran, cornflour, sweetener and milk powder into a bowl and mix together. Whisk together the egg and the yoghurt and stir into the dry ingredients.

Heat a large flat griddle or frying pan and spoon on 4 tablespoons of the mixture.

Cook for 2–3 minutes on each side and then pop in the oven for 2–3 minutes to cook through. Leave to cool on a wire rack.

Meanwhile, stir the grated lemon zest into the Greek yoghurt.

Serve the scones topped with a dollop of lemon yoghurt.

If you are in the Consolidation or Stabilization phases, serve these scones with a few strawberry slices or raspberries and some mint leaves.

ALMOND RASPBERRY CAKE

Serves 6 Preparation time: **20 minutes** Cooking time: **25 minutes**

The Dukan Diet version of a Victoria sandwich! If you want to vary the filling, just follow the instructions for making the cake and then make a filling of your choice. Cream cheese with sweetener and grated lemon or orange zest would be equally delicious and would also make this a Cruise phase recipe.

consolidation

stabilization

6 tbsp oat bran
40g cornflour
25g skimmed milk powder
1 tsp baking powder
3 tbsp sweetener
2 eggs, beaten

150g fat-free natural yoghurt
20g virtually fat-free quark
15g fat-free fromage frais
1 tsp almond essence
200g extra-light cream cheese
200g raspberries

Preheat the oven to 180°C/350°F/Gas 4. Lightly oil a 20cm cake tin and line with greaseproof paper.

In a large bowl, mix together the oat bran, cornflour, milk powder, baking powder, 2 tablespoons of the sweetener, the eggs, yoghurt, quark, fromage frais and almond essence. Pour the batter into the prepared cake tin and bake in the oven for 25 minutes.

Remove from the tin and leave to cool on a wire rack.

Mix together the remaining sweetener and the cream cheese.

Lightly mash the raspberries with a fork.

Slice the cake in half horizontally, spread the bottom half with the sweetened cream cheese and cover with the raspberries. Place the other half of the cake on top and serve cut into wedges.

BLACKBERRY SQUARES

Makes 9 Preparation time: **15 minutes** Cooking time: **20 minutes**

consolidation

stabilization

These delicious treats are perfect in late summer when you can pick fresh blackberries from the hedgerows. Enjot them for an afternoon tea treat.

6 tbsp oat bran
40g cornflour
25g skimmed milk powder
2 eggs
150g fat-free natural yoghurt

30g virtually fat-free quark
1 tsp baking powder
2 tbsp sweetener
125g blackberries

Preheat the oven to 180°C/350°F/Gas 4. Lightly oil an 18cm square cake tin and line the base with greaseproof paper.

Mix all the ingredients together in a large bowl. Don't worry about breaking up the blackberries slightly as this will give a lovely marbling effect.

Pour the mixture into the prepared tin and bake in the oven for 20 minutes until risen and golden.

Cool in the tin, and then remove and cut into nine squares.

If you are in the Stabilization phase, you can add 25g desiccated coconut to the mixture to make Blackberry and Coconut Squares.

CHOCOLATE CAKE

Serves 4 Preparation time: 15 minutes Cooking time: 18-20 minutes

It's great to know that you can still enjoy a chocolaty treat and stay true to Dukan principles. This cake is perfect for Easter or just when you fancy a bit of something sweet.

consolidation

stabilization

6 eggs, separated
3 tbsp sweetener
30g fat-reduced, sugar-free cocoa powder
50g raspberries
100g extra-light cream cheese
1–2 tbsp skimmed milk

Preheat the oven to 200°C/400°F/Gas 6. Lightly oil an 18cm oval or circular cake tin and line with greaseproof paper.

Whisk the egg whites until stiff. Whisk together the egg yolks, 2 tablespoons of the sweetener and 20g of the cocoa powder. Fold the egg whites into the egg yolk mixture and pour two thirds into the prepared circular tin.

Drop the raspberries into the middle of the mixture, then spoon over the remaining mixture. Bake in the oven for 18–20 minutes, until cooked through. Leave to cool in the tin.

Beat together the remaining sweetener, remaining cocoa powder, the cream cheese and enough milk to make the mixture of a spreading consistency.

Spread the icing over the cake and serve cut into wedges.

PEAR & GINGER MUFFINS

Makes 12 Preparation time: **15 minutes** Cooking time: **20 minutes**

 consolidation

stabilization

*Great if you want to have an afternoon treat on the diet — and this one's guilt-free!
If you don't like pears, you can use other fruits such as apples or plums.*

12 tbsp oat bran
80g cornflour
50g skimmed milk powder
4 eggs
300g fat-free natural yoghurt
60g virtually fat-free quark

2 tsp baking powder
4 tbsp sweetener
3 pears, peeled, cored and diced
2cm piece fresh root ginger, peeled
    and grated

Preheat the oven to 180°C/350°F/Gas 4. Line a 12-hole muffin tin with paper cases.

Mix all the ingredients together in a large bowl. Spoon the batter into the paper cases
and bake in the oven for 20 minutes, until risen and golden.

Cool on a wire rack. Store in an airtight container.

 ·

*Leave out the fruit completely if you are still in the Cruise phase and just add a flavouring,
such as grated orange or lemon zest or fat-reduced, sugar-free cocoa powder.*

· ·

INDEX

almonds
almond raspberry cake *245*
baked spiced passion fruit plums *213–15*
chicken korma with green pepper *101*
French almond & onion soup *71*
anchovies
chicken Caesar salad *194–5*
grilled Dover sole with salsa verde *143*
salade Niçoise *133–5*
apples
citrus baked apples *234–5*
roasted monkfish
with celeriac coleslaw *198*
apricots
carrot & orange pâté *55*
asparagus with poached egg *190*
Attack phase *6, 8, 9, 10–11*
aubergines
lentil moussaka *176–7*
ratatouille stuffed pancakes *178–9*
roast cod & ratatouille *148–9*
smoky aubergine & coriander dip *82–3*

bacon
bacon wrapped scallops *26–7*
chicken Caesar salad *194–5*
corn & bacon chowder *67–9*
cottage pie *110–11*
creamy herb stuffed chicken
breast *88–9*
English breakfast tortilla *76–7*
grilled calf's liver with Puy lentils *109*
spaghetti bolognese *120*
stir-fry beef with carrot &
Chinese cabbage *116–17*
beans
chargrilled courgette & cannellini
bean salad *164–5*
chicken & butternut casserole *95*
chump of lamb
with gremolata *124–5*
egg, ham & bean salad *80–1*
haricot bean, tuna & mint pâté *60–1*
rosemary & garlic roasted leg of
lamb *121–3*
salade Niçoise *133–5*
spiced butternut wedges
with butter bean dip *42–3*
spiced kale with flageolet beans *160*
spinach, broad bean & feta salad *50–1*
tuna & bean salad *44–5*
winter bean & tofu casserole *175*
beef
beef & mushroom goulash *112–13*
cottage pie *110–11*
Italian meatballs
with vegetable pasta *113–14*

peppered steak
with horseradish sauce *31*
spaghetti bolognese *120*
spicy beef stuffed peppers *106–7*
spicy egg topped burger
with mustard sauce *34–5*
stir-fry beef with carrot & Chinese
cabbage *116–17*
Thai beef soup *32–3*
warm cabbage salad
with seared beef *108*
beetroot
roast beetroot & spinach salad *158–9*
tofu stuffed cabbage *172–3*
blackberries
blackberry fool *238–9*
blackberry squares *248–9*
bread
cheese & onion flatbread
with houmous *46, 49*
broccoli
roast beetroot & spinach salad *158–9*
salmon & broccoli tabbouleh *196–7*
spinach stuffed sole *204*
superfood salad *78–9*
winter bean & tofu casserole *175*
butternut squash
bubble & squeak topped
with poached egg *168–9*
butternut squash & haddock soup *75*
chicken & butternut casserole *95*
cottage pie *110–11*
fish & chips *142*
pumpkin risotto *170–1*
salade Niçoise *133–5*
salmon & squash fish cakes *128–9*
spiced butternut wedges
with butter bean dip *42–3*
turkey, butternut & spinach curry *98–9*
vegetable cottage pie *174*
vegetable masala *184–5*

cabbage
bubble & squeak topped
with poached egg *168–9*
crab burgers *150–1*
curried chicken with coleslaw *102–3*
egg & vegetable fried rice *56–7*
mackerel & potato salad *130–1*
stir-fry beef with carrot & Chinese
cabbage *116–17*
tofu stuffed cabbage *172–3*
warm cabbage salad
with seared beef *108*
capers
fish & chips *142*
grilled Dover sole with salsa verde *143*

roast salmon with chickpea
& red pepper salad *152–3*
cardamom rice pudding
with roasted plums *240–1*
carrots
carrot & orange pâté *55*
curried chicken with coleslaw *102–3*
egg & vegetable fried rice *56–7*
fish & chips *142*
Italian meatballs
with vegetable pasta *113–14*
roasted monkfish
with celeriac coleslaw *198–9*
stir-fry beef with carrot &
Chinese cabbage *116–17*
vegetable cottage pie *174*
vegetable masala *184–5*
warm cabbage salad
with seared beef *108*
winter bean & tofu casserole *175*
cauliflower
cottage pie *110–11*
vegetable masala *184–5*
celeriac
roasted monkfish with celeriac
coleslaw *198–9*
chargrilled courgette & cannellini
bean salad *164–5*
cheese
almond raspberry cake *245*
asparagus with poached egg *190*
cheese & onion flatbread
with houmous *46, 49*
chicken & herb soufflé *191–3*
chicken Caesar salad *194–5*
chocolate cake *250–1*
in the Consolidation phase *14, 15*
cottage pie *110–11*
crab, tomato & saffron tart *202–3*
creamy herb stuffed chicken breast
88–9
curried chicken with coleslaw *102–3*
fish pie *146–7*
French almond & onion soup *71*
haddock Florentine *140–1*
lentil moussaka *176–7*
pepper & courgette lasagne *182–3*
polenta pizza *180–1*
pumpkin risotto *170–1*
ratatouille stuffed pancakes *178–9*
roast beetroot & spinach salad *159*
roast cod & ratatouille *148*
smoked haddock & spring onion
risotto *200*
spicy beef stuffed peppers *106–7*
spinach, broad bean & feta salad *50–1*
stuffed peaches *236–7*

tuna & lentil bake *154–5*
vegetable cottage pie *174*
chicken
    chicken & butternut casserole *95*
    chicken & herb soufflé *191–3*
    chicken & leek soup *66*
    chicken Caesar salad *194–5*
    chicken kebabs
        with watercress couscous *91–3*
    chicken korma with green pepper *101*
    creamy herb stuffed chicken breast *88–9*
    curried chicken with coleslaw *102–3*
    jerk chicken with red pepper salsa *96–7*
    spiced chicken drumsticks
        with tabbouleh *90*
    spiced marinated chicken breasts *100*
chickpeas
    cheese & onion flatbread
        with houmous *46, 49*
    roast salmon with chickpea &
        red pepper salad *152–3*
    superfood salad *78–9*
Chinese cabbage
    crab burgers *150–1*
    egg & vegetable fried rice *56–7*
    stir-fry beef with carrot & Chinese
        cabbage *116–17*
chocolate cake *250–1*
cinnamon baked egg custard *232–3*
coconut
    blackberry and coconut squares *248*
    warm cabbage salad
        with seared beef *108*
cod
    crispy cod with lemon sauce *22*
    fish & chips *142*
    fish pie *146–7*
    roast cod & ratatouille *148–9*
Consolidation phase *6, 8, 14–15*
corn & bacon chowder *67–9*
courgettes
    chargrilled courgette & cannellini
        bean salad *164–5*
    Italian meatballs
        with vegetable pasta *113–14*
    pepper & courgette lasagne *182–3*
    ratatouille stuffed pancakes *178–9*
    roast cod & ratatouille *148–9*
    vegetable spring rolls *52–3*
couscous
    chicken kebabs with watercress
        couscous *91–3*
    salmon & broccoli tabbouleh *196–7*
    spiced chicken drumsticks
        with tabbouleh *90*
crab
    crab burgers *150–1*
    crab, tomato & saffron tart *202–3*
    creamy herb stuffed chicken breast *88–9*

Cruise phase *6, 8, 9, 12–13*
cucumber
    chilled cucumber soup *70*
    gazpacho *72–3*
    roast salmon with chickpea
        & red pepper salad *152–3*
    sesame seared tuna with cucumber
        salad *206–7*
curries
    chicken korma with green pepper *101*
    curried chicken with coleslaw *102–3*
    turkey, butternut & spinach curry *98–9*
    vegetable masala *184–5*

Dover sole
    grilled Dover sole with salsa verde *143*

eggs
    asparagus with poached egg *190*
    bubble & squeak topped
        with poached egg *168–9*
    chicken & herb soufflé *191–3*
    chicken Caesar salad *194–5*
    chocolate cake *250–1*
    cinnamon baked egg custard *232–3*
    egg & vegetable fried rice *56–7*
    egg, ham & bean salad *80–1*
    English breakfast tortilla *76–7*
    gazpacho *72–3*
    haddock Florentine *140–1*
    hard boiled *47*
    kedgeree *138–9*
    mini prawn & dill quiches *40–1*
    Oriental crab omelette *132*
    rainbow frittata *161–3*
    rhubarb & ginger sorbet *226–7*
    salade Niçoise *133–5*
    Scotch eggs *47, 48*
    smoked salmon
        with chive scrambled egg *20–1*
    spicy egg topped burger
        with mustard sauce *34–5*
    sweet soufflé omelette *36–7*
English breakfast tortilla *76–7*
exercise *9, 10, 12, 16*

fennel
    pork fillet with fennel & garlic *114–15*
    rainbow frittata *161–3*
fish
    butternut squash & haddock soup *75*
    crab burgers *150–1*
    crispy cod with lemon sauce *22*
    fish & chips *142*
    fish pie *146–7*
    grilled Dover sole with salsa verde *143*
    haddock Florentine *140–1*
    kedgeree *138–9*
    mackerel & potato salad *130–1*

Oriental crab omelette *132*
red mullet & leeks en papillote *136–7*
roast cod & ratatouille *148–9*
roast salmon with chickpea &
    red pepper salad *152–3*
roasted monkfish
    with celeriac coleslaw *198–9*
salade Niçoise *133–5*
salmon & broccoli tabbouleh *196–7*
salmon & squash fish cakes *128–9*
salmon blinis *54, 70*
salmon ceviche *201*
seafood kebabs *28–9*
smoked haddock & spring onion
    risotto *200*
smoked salmon
    with chive scrambled egg *20–1*
spicy salmon broth *64–5*
spinach stuffed sole *204*
sweet potato & haddock soup *74–5*
tuna & lentil bake *154–5*
flavourings *7*

gazpacho *72–3*
ginger
    pear & ginger muffins *252*
    rhubarb & ginger sorbet *226–7*

ham
    egg, ham & bean salad *80–1*
    seared scallops with pea purée
        & ham *188–9*

ice cream *220–1*

kale
    spiced kale with flageolet beans *160*
kedgeree *138–9*
kiwi brûlée *228–9*

lamb
    chump of lamb with gremolata *124–5*
    rosemary & garlic roasted leg of
        lamb *121–3*
leeks
    chicken & leek soup *66*
    cottage pie *111*
    creamy herb stuffed chicken breast *88–9*
    fish pie *146–7*
    red mullet & leeks en papillote *136–7*
    tofu stuffed cabbage *172–3*
    winter bean & tofu casserole *175*
lemon
    cardamom rice pudding
        with roasted plums *240–1*
    chump of lamb with gremolata *124–5*
    citrus baked apples *234–5*
    crispy cod with lemon sauce *22*
    grilled Dover sole with salsa verde *143*

mackerel & potato salad *130–1*
scones *244, 247*
lemon grass & ginger mussels *23–5*
lentils
grilled calf's liver with Puy lentils *109*
lentil moussaka *176–7*
tuna & lentil bake *154–5*
vegetable cottage pie *174*
lime
kiwi brûlée *228–9*
mango mousse *218–19*
salmon ceviche *201*
liver
grilled calf's liver with Puy lentils *109*

mackerel & potato salad *130–1*
mangetout
crab burgers *150–1*
Oriental crab omelette *132*
roast beetroot & spinach salad *158–9*
mango mousse *218–19*
mini prawn & dill quiches *40–1*
mint
chilled cucumber soup & mint
soup *70*
haricot bean, tuna & mint pâté *60–1*
roast salmon with chickpea &
red pepper salad *152–3*
salmon & broccoli tabbouleh *196–7*
spiced chicken drumsticks
with tabbouleh *90*
mushrooms
beef & mushroom goulash *112–13*
chicken & butternut casserole *95*
English breakfast tortilla *76–7*
tofu stuffed cabbage *172–3*
vegetable cottage pie *174*
vegetable stir fry with marinated
tofu *166–7*
mussels
lemon grass & ginger mussels *23–5*
seafood pasta *144–5*

oat bran *7, 9, 16*
blackberry squares *248–9*
crispy cod with lemon sauce *22*
kiwi brûlée *228–9*
oat bran pancakes
with raspberry purée *212*
pear & ginger muffins *252*
scones *244, 247*
stuffed peaches *236–7*
onions
French almond & onion soup *71*
rainbow frittata *161–3*
vegetable stir fry
with marinated tofu *166–7*
orange
carrot & orange pâté *55*

citrus baked apples *234–5*
segmenting an orange *236*
spiced rhubarb compote
with orange cream *216–17*
stir-fry beef with carrot & Chinese
cabbage *116–17*
stuffed peaches *236–7*

pancakes, ratatouille stuffed *178–9*
pasta
pepper & courgette lasagne *182–3*
seafood pasta *144–5*
spaghetti bolognese *120*
pears
pear & ginger muffins *252*
pork fillet with fennel & garlic *114–15*
peas
egg & vegetable fried rice *56–7*
rainbow frittata *161*
seared scallops with pea purée
and ham **188–9**
peppers
beef & mushroom goulash *112–13*
chicken korma with green pepper *101*
crab burgers *150–1*
haricot bean, tuna & mint pâté *60–1*
jerk chicken with red pepper salsa *96–7*
lentil moussaka *176–7*
pepper & courgette lasagne *182–3*
polenta pizza *180–1*
rainbow frittata *161–3*
ratatouille stuffed pancakes *178–9*
roast cod & ratatouille *148–9*
roast salmon with chickpea & red
pepper salad *152–3*
spicy beef stuffed peppers *106–7*
superfood salad *78–9*
vegetable spring rolls *52–3*
vegetable stir fry with marinated
tofu *166–7*
pepper & courgette lasagne *182–3*
plums
baked spiced passion fruit plums *213–15*
cardamom rice pudding
with roasted plums *240–1*
plum pudding *224–5*
polenta
crab, tomato & saffron tart *202–3*
polenta pizza *180–1*
pork
Italian meatballs with vegetable
pasta *113–14*
pork fillet with fennel & garlic *114–15*
potatoes
bubble & squeak topped
with poached egg *168*
mackerel & potato salad *130–1*
prawns
fish pie *146–7*

mini prawn & dill quiches *40–1*
prawns with a spicy dip *84–5*
seafood kebabs *28–9*
seafood pasta *144–5*
pumpkin
bubble & squeak topped
with poached egg *168–9*
pumpkin risotto *170–1*
spiced pumpkin mousse *230–1*
pure proteins (PP) *8, 10*
alternating with PV *12*
protein Thursdays *9, 15, 16*

quinoa
spinach, broad bean & feta salad *50–1*

raspberries
almond raspberry cake *245*
chocolate cake *250–1*
oat bran pancakes
with raspberry purée *212*
scones *244*
ratatouille stuffed pancakes *178–9*
red mullet & leeks en papillote *136–7*
rhubarb
rhubarb & ginger sorbet *226–7*
spiced rhubarb compote
with orange cream *216–17*
rice
egg & vegetable fried rice *56–7*
kedgeree *138–9*
pumpkin risotto *170–1*
smoked haddock & spring onion
risotto *200*

saffron
crab, tomato & saffron tart *202–3*
salads
chargrilled courgette & cannellini
bean salad *164–5*
chicken Caesar salad *194–5*
egg, ham & bean salad *80–1*
roast beetroot & spinach salad *158–9*
roast salmon with chickpea & red
pepper salad *152–3*
salade Niçoise *133–5*
sesame seared tuna
with cucumber salad *206–7*
superfood salad *78–9*
tuna & bean salad *44–5*
warm cabbage salad
with seared beef *108*
salmon
fish pie *146–7*
roast salmon with chickpea & red
pepper salad *152–3*
salmon & broccoli tabbouleh *196–7*
salmon & squash fish cakes *128–9*
salmon blinis *54, 70*

smoked salmon with chive
     scrambled egg 20–1
spicy salmon broth 64–5
sausages
     English breakfast tortilla 76–7
     Scotch eggs 47, 48
scallops
     bacon wrapped scallops 26–7
     seafood kebabs 28–9
     seared scallops with pea purée
          and ham 188–9
scones 244
Scotch eggs 47, 48
seafood kebabs 28–9
seafood pasta 144–5
sesame seared tuna
     with cucumber salad 206–7
smoked haddock
     butternut squash & haddock soup 75
     kedgeree 138–9
     smoked haddock & spring onion
          risotto 200
     sweet potato & haddock soup 74–5
smoked mackerel
     superfood salad 78–9
smoked salmon
     salmon blinis 54
     smoked salmon with chive
          scrambled egg 20–1
sole
     grilled Dover sole with salsa verde 143
     spinach stuffed sole 204
soups
     butternut squash & haddock soup 75
     chicken & leek soup 66
     chilled cucumber soup & mint
          soup 70
     corn & bacon chowder 67–9
     French almond & onion soup 71
     gazpacho 72–3
     spicy salmon broth 64–5
     sweet potato & haddock soup 74–5
spaghetti
     seafood pasta 144–5
     spaghetti bolognese 120
spiced butternut wedges
     with butter bean dip 42–3
spiced chicken drumsticks with
     tabbouleh 90
spiced kale with flageolet beans 160
spiced marinated chicken breasts 100
spicy egg topped burger
     with mustard sauce 34–5
spicy salmon broth 64–5
spinach
     fish pie 146–7
     grilled calf's liver with Puy lentils 109
     haddock Florentine 140–1
     kedgeree 138–9
     red mullet & leeks en papillote 136–7

roast beetroot & spinach salad 158–9
spinach, broad bean & feta salad 50–1
spinach stuffed sole 204
superfood salad 78–9
turkey, butternut & spinach curry
     98–9
spring onions
     bubble & squeak topped with
poached
egg 168–9
     cheese & onion flatbread
          with houmous 46, 49
     egg & vegetable fried rice 56–7
     sweetcorn & onion fritters 58–9
     vegetable spring rolls 52–3
Stabilization phase 6, 9, 16
strawberries
     Eton mess 210–11
     scones 244
     strawberry shortcake 222–3
stuffed peaches 236–7
superfood salad 78–9
swede
     cottage pie 111
sweet potatoes
     sweet potato & haddock soup 74–5
sweetcorn
     corn & bacon chowder 67–9
     sweetcorn & onion fritters 58–9

tarragon
     asparagus with poached egg 190
     bacon wrapped scallops 26–7
     chicken & herb soufflé 191–3
     spinach stuffed sole 204
Thai beef soup 32–3
tofu
     ice cream 220–1
     tofu stuffed cabbage 172–3
     vegetable stir fry
          with marinated tofu 166–7
     winter bean & tofu casserole 175
tolerated foods 13, 16
tomatoes
     chump of lamb with gremolata 124–5
     crab burgers 150–1
     crab, tomato & saffron tart 202–3
     English breakfast tortilla 76–7
     gazpacho 72–3
     rosemary & garlic roasted leg of
          lamb 121–3
     salade Niçoise 133–5
     spiced chicken drumsticks
          with tabbouleh 90
     superfood salad 78–9
     turkey burgers with tomato salsa 94
True Weight 9, 14
tuna
     haricot bean, tuna & mint pâté 60–1
     salade Niçoise 133–5

sesame seared tuna
     with cucumber salad 206–7
tuna & bean salad 44–5
tuna & lentil bake 154–5
turkey
     herb turkey escalopes 30
     Oriental turkey burgers
          with tomato salsa 94
     turkey, butternut & spinach curry
          98–9

vegetables
     and the Cruise phase 12, 13
     egg & vegetable fried rice 56–7
     Italian meatballs
          with vegetable pasta 113–14
     smoky aubergine & coriander dip 82–3
     vegetable cottage pie 174
     vegetable masala 184–5
     vegetable spring rolls 52–3
     vegetable stir fry
          with marinated tofu 166–7
venison burgers 205

walking 9, 10, 12, 16
warm cabbage salad with seared beef
     108
water 7, 10
watercress
     chicken kebabs with watercress
          couscous 91–3
weight loss
     Attack phase 10
     Cruise phase 12

yoghurt
     blackberry fool 238–9
     blackberry squares 248–9
     chicken korma with green pepper 101
     cinnamon baked egg custard 232–3
     Eton mess 210–11
     kedgeree 138–9
     kiwi brûlée 228–9
     oat bran pancakes with raspberry
          purée 212
     pear & ginger muffins 252
     plum pudding 224–5
     roasted monkfish with celeriac
          coleslaw 198–9
     scones 244
     seared scallops with pea purée &
          ham 188–9
     smoky aubergine & coriander dip 82–3
     spiced butternut wedges with herb
          and yoghurt dip 42
     spiced rhubarb compote
          with orange cream 216–17
     strawberry shortcake 222–3
     turkey, butternut & spinach curry 98–9
     vegetable masala 184–5